So You Want to Mov

Your Guide to Successful Relocation in the Mayan Riviera

Expatriate and Escape the Rat Race!

An Expat Fever™ Series Book

Defiant Press, Elk Grove, CA

Defiant Press

Author: Manny Serrato

Note: No website or company has paid a fee in order to be mentioned in this book. All the information in this book is intended for educational purposes only and cannot be considered legal advice. Expats and those considering expatriation should consult professional legal and tax advisors if they have any questions.

So You Want to Move to Playa del Carmen? Your Guide to Successful Relocation in the Mayan Riviera, Expatriate and Escape the Rat Race!

Copyright Notice. ©Defiant Press, 2015.

ISBN: 978-1-937361-17-4

Find out more about Expat Fever at our official website: www.expatfever.com.

Table of Contents

More Expat Fever! Books

Expat Fever! Relocation Guides

*So You Want To Move To **Playa Del Carmen**?*

*So You Want To Move To **Tulum**?*

*So You Want To Move To **Costa Rica**? (coming soon!)*

*So You Want To Move To **Thailand**? (coming soon!)*

"Interview with an Expat" Information Guides

*Interview with an Expat: **Playa Del Carmen, Mexico**: Learn About the Mayan Riviera from Real Expats!*

*Interview with an Expat: **Tulum, Mexico**: Learn About the Mayan Riviera from Real Expats!*

*Interview with an Expat: Costa Rica: Learn About **Costa Rica** from Real Expats! (coming soon!)*

*Interview with an Expat: Thailand: Learn About **Thailand** from Real Expats! (coming soon!)*

Are You Ready for a Major Lifestyle Change?

The *Expat Fever* series is designed to give readers a candid view of what life is like for expats living overseas. The series is also meant to provide useful advice for those considering living in another country and is written from the perspective of real expats, who know exactly what the process of expatriation is like.

This particular book discusses the Riviera Maya and more specifically, the city of Playa del Carmen.

In today's world, expatriating is now a realistic option for many people, and one of the most popular destinations for expats is Mexico. With so many people moving to Mexico, there must be something special about it!

Europeans, Canadians, and Americans are flocking to Mexico for a number of reasons. Some go for the warmer weather, while others are attracted by its close proximity to their original country. According to Mexican immigration statistics, more than 5 million expats are estimated to be living permanently in Mexico.

When asked about what attracts them to the area, nearly all expats in Playa del Carmen mention the friendly people, the environment, the laid-back lifestyle, the beautiful coastal scenery, and the relatively low cost of living. Essentially, they all say, "It's the people! It's the place! It's the fun!"

Whatever their individual reasons, more and more Americans (and people in general) are leaving their homes and their work behind to start new lives in the Riviera Maya. If you are interested in following in their footsteps by starting the next chapter of your life in paradise but aren't quite sure how to get there, then just keep reading!

Interview with an Expat: The Joys of Living in Playa

Q: We're speaking with Valerie Grant, an expat who has lived continuously in Mexico for many years. Please tell us a little bit about yourself. How did you end up in Playa del Carmen?

Valerie: I initially came to Mexico to teach English when I was 19 years old. I bought a ticket from Vancouver and stepped off the plane with an overstuffed backpack, some rudimentary knowledge of Spanish numbers, and a notebook jammed with contact information for all the local English schools.

I've now been based out of Mexico for just over 5 years. My original plan was to come to Playa del Carmen, stay for a few months, and then travel south to Argentina. An unexpected series of events changed that plan. I quickly fell in love with the people, the food, and the culture of Playa, and I'm so happy to be a full-time resident here.

I currently live in a quirky, off-the-grid eco-village called Pueblo SacBe. It's about a 15 minute drive from downtown Playa. As soon as I turn off the highway, I enter a lush green oasis that is home to group of offbeat individuals from around the world. Like the people who live here, SacBe is almost impossible to describe. It's a sustainable eco-development, where the gravel roads are lined with Dali sculptures. It's a place where people swim in the clear waters of the surrounding cenotes and where people from all walks of life can come together to live in harmony and to respect the environment. SacBe also has dozens of rustic hiking trails and, we even have our own amphitheater and music festival!

My personal home is basically a sort of modern treehouse. It runs on solar power and is guarded by my rescue pups.

Q: Could you tell us about how you decided to expatriate and what exactly drew you to this area?

Valerie: I wanted to live near the beach, but I wasn't prepared to leave the comforts of civilization. I enjoy ice-cold beers and socializing way too much not to live near a city. For me, Playa was the perfect compromise.

Playa is perched on the edge of the Caribbean Sea, and it's surrounded by Mayan Ruins and lush jungle. Being able to enjoy such fantastic scenery is important to me, but I still have easy access to all the comforts of home—I can even drive to a Walmart if I need to.

Quintana Roo (which is the Mexican state where Playa located) has lots of small towns. They all have a lot to offer, but Playa is by far the best place to expatriate, especially if great schools and places to work are important to you.

Q: Do you feel that Playa is a good place to raise kids?

Valerie: It's funny that you ask that. To be honest, I was never a big fan of kids until I moved to Playa. The children of SacBe are incredible— inquisitive, creative, and full of life. It's not uncommon to see them feeding the turtles down in the cenotes or building forts in the bushes. The kids here are so happy. I think that Playa is a perfect place to raise a family. The atmosphere here is so warm and welcoming, and there's a real sense of community among the people.

I taught at a bilingual pre-school for a short period of time, and I was always astonished at how quickly little ones can adapt to new surroundings. Children would arrive having never spoken a work or Spanish in their lives, and a few days later, they would be leading the games at recess and jabbering away in "Spanglish."

There is just so much education outside of the classroom here in Playa too. Kids can learn about sea creatures as they swim in the ocean, and they can study history while climbing ancient ruins.

Plus, Mexico has a very family focused culture. Families and neighbors really support one another here, and people are always willing to lend a helping hand to those who need one.

Q: There is a lot of tourism in the Riviera Maya. How can a person from a different country come to live and work here? What is the local economy like?

Valerie: There is a lot of tourism here, but Playa is a lot less Americanized than some of the bigger tourist destinations in the area. A lot of people like to define Playa as the "Anti-Cancun," but there's more to it than that.

To me, the real difference is that Playa takes a bit more of a natural approach to tourism. When you walk down the streets of Playa, you know that you are still in Mexico. Yes, there are giant resorts along the beach, but there are also lots of smaller boutique hotels and even some family-run guest homes.

A lot of expats end up working the hospitality industry. There are also a number of niche markets here in Playa, including wild eco-tourism adventures and specialized health services for medical tourists.

There is also a trend now, where a lot of expats are developing locally based start-ups here. While Mexico still has fairly conservative lending policies, there are incredible opportunities here for just about anyone with a good idea and a plan.

Though I started here as a teacher, I have worked in a number of different fields since moving here. Most recently, I started my own business in the area of ecological architecture and sustainable building. It took a lot of work and research for me to get where I am, but Playa has definitely opened a lot of doors for me.

Q: What are some examples of the kind of culture shock that an expat might experience here?

Valerie: One of the first things that really threw me for a loop here were the Mexican nicknames! When someone called me *gordita* ("a little fat"), I thought they were insulting me. It wasn't until later that I realized that the term is often used in an endearing way.

A lot of Mexican nicknames seem derogatory when translated literally into English, but they are generally said with a specific kind of tongue-in-cheek affection. If you have any physical characteristics that stand out, expect people to pick up on them! When they do, take everything with a sense of humor; there's no use getting upset if one of the neighbors calls you a *pelon* ("bald man").

Q: How are foreigners viewed in Playa?

Valerie: I don't really feel that there are any specific prejudices or targeted negativity against foreigners here. People treat expats as individuals, and if you treat the locals with dignity and respect, then they will probably reciprocate. The stereotype of the "ugly *gringo*"— someone who waltzes in and announces complains loudly in English— is alive and well in Playa, and the best way to avoid negative attention is to be polite and respectful.

Due to negative experiences with tourists in the past, it is understandable why some locals might sometimes be reluctant to listen to people who are new to the area. Locals also don't really want to hear about how things are different or better in the US. Don't pass judgement until you have spent enough time here to really know the people and the culture.

For the most part though, locals in Playa are incredibly friendly. This is a great place to get to know people and make friends. It's not at all strange for a quick run to the *tiendita* to take 30 minutes longer than it should, because one of the locals wants to share all the latest neighborhood gossip.

Q: Many people think that Mexico is dangerous. How do you feel about security and the police in Playa? Is it a safe place to live?

Valerie: I've never felt like I had any reason to worry about organized crime or drug activity here in Playa.

My greatest personal concern is petty crime, but using a little common sense goes along way. As long as you don't do things like leave valuables in the car or ignore your surroundings, you should be just fine. If you ever do see something suspicious, the best thing to do is to tell your neighbors and the police.

Many private developments and buildings in Playa have hired security guards or are under informal neighborhood watch programs, both of which deter crime and help people feel safe.

Police in Mexico have a bad rap. Yes, there is definitely some corruption on the force, but that doesn't change the fact that many of the police truly are dedicated to keeping people safe.

 When interacting with the police, I recommend that expats stay calm and keep a level head. For example, if you get pulled over, don't agree to pay any bribes; just request an official ticket instead. More often than not, the officer won't want to go through all the paperwork and will just let you go.

A lot of people may not realize it, but one of the best ways to stay safe is to learn Spanish and stay informed. Playa is a safe place, and a little caution and awareness goes a long way.

Q: What is some advice that you can give to someone who wants to experience life as a local?

Valerie: Well, if you are planning to just spend all your time here lying in a hammock on the beach, think again. There is always something going on here. The locals are very active.

During a typical week, you can find me practicing yoga, volunteering at an orphanage, belly dancing with my friends, attending a tequila tasting with my colleagues, and a lot more.

Since there is such a dizzying array of things to do here, the best way to experience life as a local is to do what interests you.

For example, if you're a foodie, take a stroll down 5th Avenue to explore the restaurants and befriend their owners. If sports are your thing, go scuba diving, fishing, or kite surfing.

Sometimes, we expats struggle to learn Spanish, because so many of the locals already speak English, but knowing the language makes it much easier to feel like a local and experience Playa in the most authentic way. I recommend taking a course or participating in one of the many free conversation clubs to hone your language skills. Language classes are also a great way to meet people.

Playa del Carmen also offers a lot of opportunities to give back to the community, which is a great way connect with the locals. Local shelters for women and children are always in need of assistance, and the turtle sanctuaries always welcome a helping hand. A number of global groups have chapters in Playa, including Rotary and the Red Cross.

Mexico is also famous for its parties, and the easiest way to live like a local is to celebrate like a local! Getting involved with local holidays and celebrations is a great way to become integrated with the culture.

Oh, and if you are ever lucky enough to be in Playa during a World Cup year, be prepared for one of the biggest parties of your life! The city shuts down, and the streets are filled with people.

Q: How do you keep in touch with family back home?

Valerie: Social media keeps me updated on everyone up north. I share a lot of pictures of what I see here and post a lot of stories about my experiences, which help my family feel more connected to me. I also use Skype to chat with people on a fairly regular basis. I have a Canadian phone number connected to my Skype account, so friends and family can also call me locally if they want. When I do finally get to see people in person, I never really feel like anything has changed, and we always pick up right where we left off.

One of the advantages of living in Playa is that you have easy access to Cancun's airport, which makes it pretty simple to fly to most major destinations in the US and Canada. Of course, since Playa is so beautiful, most of your family back home will probably want to come visit you themselves, so get a place with a guest room!

Q. Could you tell us a bit about your move and your visa choices?

Valerie: Sure. Legally speaking, I am a temporary resident of Mexico. This is the next step up from a visitor's visa. One of the most important things to do if you move here is to legalize your immigration status, especially since you can't sign a rental agreement or open a local bank account if you don't.

I've been through the immigration process a few times. When I first moved down to Playa, it was possible to "change" my immigration status from within Mexico's borders. I was issued a tourist visa upon arrival at the airport, got hired by a school shortly thereafter, and they sponsored me for an FM3 (a Mexican work visa). All I had to do was make some copies, pay a modest fee, and take a few trips down to the immigration offices. It was a fairly simple process, and I was able to complete the application without any assistance from lawyers.

Things have changed since then though. Immigration laws in Mexico were reformed both in 2012 and in 2014, and it is no longer possible to change your tourist visa to any other kind of visa while you are in Mexico. Instead, you have to apply at a Mexican consulate in your home country and meet all the various eligibility requirements.

In my case, I was able to obtain a temporary residence visa based on economic solvency. Essentially, that means that I am "sponsoring" myself and that I have sufficient monthly income to sustain my lifestyle in Mexico.

I was issued a temporary residency visa in Canada after a lengthy interview at the consulate. Once I flew back to Mexico, I had to go to the offices in Cancun within 30 days, pay a fee, and show some more paperwork before I eventually received an official *residente temporal* card.

I was able to complete the process on my own, but I have heard horror stories from other expats who weren't so lucky. The consulate staff in Canada were extremely helpful; not only did they answer all of my questions, they also gave me a lot of tips for speeding things along. I felt confident in completing the application on my own, but my case was fairly straightforward. If anyone has any doubts about the process, the best thing for them to do is speak with a lawyer.

Q: Do you have any other advice for dealing with the recent reforms in Mexico?

Valerie: Regulations governing many aspects of expat life have changed in recent years. The procedures for importing a vehicle, opening a bank account, paying off your credit card, legalizing your car, and crossing the border with a pet are some of the things that have been affected.

Expats should always do their research and look at several sources. There are many online forums in English that are great for getting answers to questions about moving here. There are also great print resources like *The Yucatan Times*.

Unfortunately, there are a number of scam artists operating in Playa del Carmen, and new expats are sometimes seen as easy targets for fraud. Mexico doesn't have the same governing bodies or organizations that many of us are accustomed to north of the border, so it pays to ask around and do your research before entrusting someone with your financial details or personal information. Ask for personal recommendations and always take the time to search for people and businesses online before working with them.

This is a little off topic, but another really good thing to know is that color copies of official documents are illegal. I learned this the hard way—from my lawyer after an incident with the traffic police. If you need a certified copy of an immigration document or driver's license, get a simple black and white copy and take it to a notary. By law, all foreigners need to carry documents to prove that they are legally present in Mexico. Obviously, carrying the original copies of your immigration papers to the beach isn't all that smart, so certified copies are a must.

Q. Thank you so much for talking with us! This last question is pretty general. Can you tell us your honest opinion of the area and share any last advice you have for someone moving to Playa?

Valerie: I'll start with the second part first. My advice is simple: take the leap! Some people might think that it's a little extreme to move to another country, but if you are already thinking about moving to Playa, go ahead and give it a try!

Of course, before fully committing to moving here, it's a good idea to get to know the place. Take a time off, and give yourself at least a month to spend exploring Playa and getting to know its various neighborhoods. There are lots of short-term rentals here, and it's pretty easy to arrange for accommodations through sites like Airbnb. Keep an eye out for furnished apartment rentals while you're here too.

As for my opinion of the city, well, it's certainly a positive one! As I often tell people, it's impossible to be bored in Playa! The city always feels new and exciting, and I feel more liberated and alive here than I ever did back in Canada. I really can't imagine a better place than my home here in SacBe.

Why Choose Playa del Carmen?

If you're reading this guide, then you're probably thinking of moving to Playa del Carmen. Playa del Carmen is a lovely place for a vacation, but will the city suit your personality in the long-term? Are you prepared to embrace a new city and a new culture?

Close your eyes and imagine yourself in Playa del Carmen. Are you ready to change your life and learn how to live like the locals do? Adventure is there for the taking—all you have to do is step out and embrace it.

What are your reasons for wanting to move to Mexico, and are those reasons good enough for you leave your current lifestyle behind?

Every person who relocates to the city has their own unique set of reasons for saying goodbye to their US address. Many like the fact that US citizens can automatically receive a 6-month visa upon arrival. Some people are motivated by job offers or business opportunities, while others are simply looking for something new. Every expat has their own story to tell.

If you still have some doubts about your decision to expatriate, the information about Playa del Carmen below should make it much easier for you to make up your mind.

It's Always Sunny in Playa del Carmen

The weather in Playa del Carmen is perfect for anyone who hates cold winters or long rainy seasons. In fact, the wonderful weather is one of the primary reasons that so many people move to Playa del Carmen. The sun is almost always shining in the Riviera Maya, so it's no wonder that the people in Playa del Carmen tend to be warmer and friendlier than in other parts of the world—it's almost impossible not to smile when the sun is shining and the birds are singing.

There are not many rainy days in Playa (which is what the locals call it), which means that you can easily spend most of your time there enjoying the outdoors. While there is a hurricane season to deal with, not every day during that season is rainy or stormy. On the contrary, the skies remain sunny and clear most of the time. Storms are the exception, not the rule, and if there ever is a hurricane, most structures in the area are built to keep everyone safe.

The hottest month in Playa is May, when the average high temperature is about 90°. The coldest month is January, when the high is often in the 60s. For the rest of the year, temperatures tend to range from the 60s and 70s to the 80s and 90s. Even when it rains (most often in September and October), the temperatures remain pleasant.

A Modern City Plus a Tranquil Beach Resort

Another aspect of Playa that draws many expats is the quality of its beaches. The area's spectacular strips of white sand are caressed by the stunning and wonderfully relaxing waves of the Caribbean Sea.

Playa del Carmen's beautiful beaches draw a large amount of tourists annually, but don't let the crowds and the 5-star resorts deter you from relocating there. While there is a tourist presence in Playa, there are plenty of quieter and more isolated spots for the locals to enjoy. If you aren't a fan of crowds, try having lunch at one of the restaurants outside of the tourist area (which is along 5th Avenue or *Quinta Avenida*) or strike up a conversation with some locals. If you open your heart to Playa and take the time to experience it as a local, then it's sure to win you over. Many expats in the area started as tourists who just couldn't stop themselves from making permanent homes in this remarkable city.

25 years ago, Playa del Carmen was a small fishing village inhabited by only a few dozen families. The city was just a stopover for travelers visiting Cozumel Island. But today, Playa del Carmen is one of the fastest growing cities in Latin America, and it offers many opportunities for investors and developers.

Today's Playa still has the charm of the small fishing village that it once was, but it is also a lively city that's rich in culture and history. And while Playa del Carmen has beaches and waters as beautiful as those in Cancun, it's also less crowded and more inviting.

The Low Cost of Living

Another one of the top reasons that US citizens decide to move to Playa del Carmen is the low cost of living and the fact that the city offers fantastic options for any budget.

Food and housing are cheaper in Mexico than they are in America. At the same time, transportation, services, and utilities are also more affordable.

While gas is about $3.50 per gallon in Mexico, water is only about $6 per month, and it's not too difficult to find a 2-bedroom apartment near the beach for just $900 per month. A 3-bedroom home with a pool that's close to the beach will cost you about $1,500 per month, and a studio apartment a few miles from the beach might cost as little as $200 a month.

Tip! Rent is very cheap in rural areas, but tourist areas are sometimes just as expensive as the US, especially if you want a fancy villa or a luxury oceanfront condo. Generally speaking, real estate gets cheaper the further from the beach you go. If you are looking to save some money, try to find a home or apartment in a more secluded area away from the water. A few miles from the beach makes a huge difference in price.

Fresh foods like vegetables, grains, fish, and eggs are also surprisingly cheap in Playa del Carmen, so if you want to save money on food, stay away from the tourist traps and just eat like the locals do. If you don't want to cook for yourself, you can get a complete meal for just 50 pesos (about $4) in most local restaurants.

A Welcoming Environment with Modern Amenities

Playa del Carmen's modern amenities make it easy for expats to adjust and feel at home. While the scenery, people, and lifestyle are different than what many are used to, the general atmosphere is relatively familiar, and the abundance of expats makes it easy for newcomers to feel at home. English is also widely spoken in the city, and the expat communities are large and welcoming.

While many move to Playa so that they can slow down a bit, others choose to stay busy. Whether you want to focus on work or want to immerse yourself in more relaxing hobbies, there is no shortage of things to do or of people to connect with in Playa del Carmen.

Proximity to the US

Playa del Carmen is located about 50 miles from Cancun at the center of the Riviera Maya, which runs from south of Cancun to Tulum. The city's convenient location makes it easy for residents to access Cancun International Airport, which offers multiple daily flights to more than 20 cities in the US and to 7 in Canada.

If you make the decision to move to Playa, you won't have to worry about finding a way to make it home for the holidays or other special occasions. If you ever need to return to your loved ones quickly, all you have to do is hop on a plane for a few hours.

What's Your Motivation for Moving?

While you're probably excited about living in a different country, meeting new people, admiring new scenery, and broadening your horizons, it's not a good idea to rush into expatriation. Before taking the plunge and moving to a new country, it's important to consider your decision from multiple angles.

Before you start telling everyone that you're moving or quitting your day job, ask yourself a few questions about yourself and your reasons for relocating.

Are You Ready to Leave Loved Ones Behind?

This is probably the toughest question to ask somebody who is planning to move in a new country. No matter how compelling their reasons for relocating, most people are never quite ready to leave their family and friends.

While things like Skype and Facebook make it easier than ever for people to stay in touch across long distances, you have to figure out whether that will be enough for you. You can always make new friends in Playa (and you should), but getting close to new people takes a while. Starting over socially and overcoming feelings of isolation are some of the hardest parts of becoming an expat. The rewards of relocation can be great in the long-term, but not everyone is ready for that sort of challenge.

What About Your Spouse and Children?

Sometimes a spouse or partner is unable to adapt to their new lifestyle. So before you decide to relocate to Mexico, make sure that everyone is truly on board with your plans. Is your spouse putting their own career on hold for you to embrace this opportunity? Are they going to be able to live with this decision without feeling frustrated? Such questions have to be answered before you can move. If you are bringing loved ones with you to Playa, don't forget that your happiness and wellbeing is intertwined with theirs.

If you have children and you're taking them with you, then you need to find a good school (that you can afford) and make sure that they will be able to adjust to their new home. You should also consider the fact that good schooling tends to be rather expensive abroad.

Can You Handle the Culture Shock?

Leaving the US means saying goodbye to more than your family and friends. You also have to get used to the idea of holidays like the Fourth of July and Thanksgiving not being celebrated by most of the people around you. You can still celebrate such holidays privately, but it won't feel the same. In Playa del Carmen, people will celebrate things like Benito Juarez's Birthday and the Day of the Dead, and you will need to adapt to this.

Although it might seem like nothing now, you also need to be prepared to say goodbye to some of your favorite foods, English-language magazines, movies, and much more. Finding such things in Playa del Carmen may be impossible, or they may be terribly expensive. In fact, you will probably have to change many of your usual recipes to use what's available, and you may also need to seek out new forms of pop culture to enjoy.

You may also find that locals in Playa see the world a little differently than most new expats. This isn't necessarily a bad thing, but relocating abroad does require you to be able to stop comparing and start embracing. You may not always like or understand everything you encounter in Playa del Carmen, but you probably don't like everything about your current home either. What's important is that you find a way to embrace the culture in front of you despite its flaws and that you don't let your old experiences and expectations prevent you from becoming a member of your new community.

If you ever move abroad, take the time to learn as much as you can about the local history, social customs, holidays, festivities, and other traditions. You should also make sure to learn how you are expected to behave in social situations involving non-expats.

Do You Want to Retire There or Just Visit?

Planning an indefinite stay in Playa del Carmen is complicated, especially when old age comes into play. Before moving, you need to think very carefully about taxes, social security, and retirement benefits. Depending on your agreements, choosing to expatriate might actually cause you to lose the benefits promised in your home country. If you are a US resident and you move to Mexico, you will also lose certain annuity income and tax-advantages.

Before moving, examine your pension and savings plans and consult an accountant or attorney in the US who can help you better understand the system in Mexico.

You should also learn all you can about the Mexican health care system and take all the necessary steps to secure health insurance.

Are You Ready to Create a New Life?

If you take yourself too seriously, then you probably should not consider moving to a new country. There will be a lot of trial and error with the new language, the new culture, and the new community, and you have to be prepared to take new experiences as they come. The success of your transition depends on how well you learn from, adapt to, and embrace the new situations that you find yourself in, so make sure you pack your sense of humor you when you go.

Tip! Don't compare the way things are done in Mexico to the way things are done "back home." Be flexible, and accept that some things will be done differently. If you do, you'll enjoy your stay a whole lot more.

Playa del Carmen: Pros and Cons

Before deciding to move to Playa del Carmen, you need to understand that expatriating is not just an extended vacation in some exotic corner of the world. In fact, once the honeymoon phase ends, you may find that there are some things you don't like about your new home.

If you find that you just can't live without moving at a hectic pace with a coffee in one hand and a cell phone in the other, then Playa del Carmen might not be the best place for you. No one moves to Playa to wear a suit and carry a briefcase! They move to Playa to enjoy life and to live more peacefully.

Knowing a thing or two about Playa del Carmen will help you understand the community and the locals on a deeper level and will help you decide if it's the right city for you.

Location and Size

Playa del Carmen is situated on the Yucatan Peninsula, in the state of Quintana Roo on the Caribbean coast. This small corner of paradise is part of the Riviera Maya, a stretch of land between Cancun and Tulum that is known for its 5-star resorts and beautiful beaches. Though it is loved by tourists, Playa has an authentic Mexican aura and a relaxing small town feel. Playa also has a more rustic vibe than Cancun, which tends to be more fast-paced and consumer-driven.

Playa del Carmen has gained a lot of popularity in the last two decades, and today, it is the second largest Mexican resort destination (after Cancun). Playa is also the fastest growing city in Mexico; the city is home to about 180,000 people and has a flourishing tourism industry.

Daily life in Playa del Carmen is quite different from the "hustle and bustle" of regular city life. Life in this beautiful beach city is wonderfully tranquil, but it can be a little difficult for some to adjust to it at first.

There are no traffic jams in Playa del Carmen. There are no morning coffee runs or quick trips to McDonald's either. Generally speaking, the city offers a relaxing environment that keeps stress at bay.

Those who live in Playa love to enjoy every moment that they have there. They usually wake up early to enjoy breakfast (or even a quick swim) before going to work. Even for those with jobs, every day feels like the weekend in this spectacular city. People in Playa del Carmen laugh more, live more, and work less, so it's no surprise that they also tend to be easygoing and happy.

Life in Playa involves plenty of time dedicated to outdoor fun, fitness, yoga, meeting with friends, discovering new cultures, and relaxing on the beach. Leaving the fast-paced American rat race behind in order to dedicate more of your time to enjoying life truly is a rewarding experience.

Of course, there is more to life than relaxing in the sand. You will have to adapt to a new culture and a new way of thinking.

City Life: The Pros

Life in Playa del Carmen moves at a slower pace. The city offers an idyllic setting for relaxation and entices people to do things like take slow walks along the beach and admire the sunset while shopping. Locals and expats love going to the beach, especially outside of the peak tourism season, when the sands are quieter and the ambience more peaceful.

Many expats find that moving to Playa del Carmen allows them to spend more time engaging in activities like tennis, golf, snorkeling, scuba diving, sea kayaking, fishing, sailing, surfing, and yoga. Water activities are particularly popular because of the Caribbean Sea's spectacular turquoise waters and amazing coral reefs.

Playa is also only a stone's throw away from the beautiful Mayan ruins of Coba, Tulum, and Chichen Itza. The city is also in the vicinity of the fascinating flora and fauna of Sian Ka'an Biosphere Reserve.

Although Playa del Carmen is a modern city, the locals have taken precautions to keep its local charm alive and well. For example, new buildings can't be more than 3 stories tall, so you won't find any suffocating sky scrapers in the city. The locals don't want Playa to become the next Cancun, a city that has lost its traditional aura.

As welcoming as it is to newcomers, Playa del Carmen is also distinctly Mexican. It's a place where you can still find family-run *tienditas* (small local stores) and where local plumbers and carpenters still advertise their services on the street. Playa del Carmen has transformed itself from a sleepy fishing village into a world-class resort town without sacrificing its local roots, authenticity, or traditions.

City Life: Cons

The slower pace of life in Mexico (and especially in smaller cities like Playa del Carmen) is attractive to many expats. At the same time, some expats become frustrated when they realize that punctuality is not exactly the locals' strongest quality.

If you hear a local say *"mañana"* in Playa del Carmen, they aren't necessarily referring to "tomorrow." In fact, they probably just mean "sometime in the future." Responses to emails and phone calls are often delayed, because people don't consider them urgent and prefer to interact in person. No amount of prodding or grumbling will change the fact that time works a little differently in Playa, so go with the flow and find a way to adapt to the slower lifestyle.

One of the best things about Mexican culture is that Mexicans are always ready to give a helping hand. The locals just can't say no to someone in distress. While this is usually a good thing, it often causes unexpected delays. For example, if you take your car to the mechanic and return to get it the next day, you might find that it isn't ready, because your mechanic has been busy helping others on more urgent matters. Eventually, you will get used to such delays and will come to understand that they are just a part of life in Playa.

Tip! If you find a good handyman, hang on to him! Don't worry if he tends to arrive a little bit late either. It can be hard to find trustworthy plumbers, electricians, and carpenters in Playa del Carmen, so it's best to keep a friendly relationship with them once you find them. Be patient, and remember that tardiness isn't seen as much of a problem to locals.

Tropical Weather: Pros

As mentioned before, the fantastic weather is one of the reasons that many people choose to move Playa del Carmen. Even during the winter months, most days are warm and sunny, and nights are refreshing and pleasant. It's a real tropical paradise, and you will never have to experience freezing winters, shoveling snow from your vehicle, or chopping firewood for the fireplace or buck stove.

Tropical Weather: Cons

If you aren't used to a tropical climate, then you may find some of your time in Playa to be uncomfortably hot. It takes most newcomers some time to adapt to the climate and to accept they will be sweaty for most of the summer. Humidity is also pretty high in Playa del Carmen, but the ocean breeze does provide some relief.

The rainy season starts in April and lasts until July. Tropical storms in Playa are usually short and localized, but can be quite a nuisance.

Hurricane season starts in June and continues through November, but it is possible for hurricanes to form any time of year. Living in Playa del Carmen means getting used to hurricanes, which occur most often during August, September, and October (this period coincides with the tourism down season).

While you might be worried about hurricanes, most of the region's storms are not destructive. In fact, in the last 40 years, only 4 damaging hurricanes have impacted Playa del Carmen. Moreover, most of the newer buildings in the city are built to withstand hurricanes.

If you are ever instructed to prepare for a hurricane, don't wait until the last minute to purchase supplies. Since hurricanes can disrupt gas, electricity, water, and telephone services, make sure to have everything you need to survive for a few days.

Tip! Despite all this talk about hurricanes, the biggest weather-related problem facing tourists is actually sunburn. Make sure you wear a strong sunscreen, a hat, and sunglasses whenever you go outside in the sun. You should also carry a pocket-sized raincoat with you for any surprise summer rains.

Diversity in a Resort Town: Pros

Playa del Carmen is inhabited by two main groups, the "locals" and the "expats."

Because Playa del Carmen is home to people of many different nationalities and to a growing expat community, the community there is very diverse and people tend to accept that not everyone is the same. The fact that there are so many different kinds of people in the city means that residents have the opportunity to learn about many cultures and are free to make their own decisions without worrying about others judging them for their difference. Many of those who have moved to Playa in last 10 years have done so, because they want to live in the friendly and accepting community that the city offers.

Diversity in a Resort Town: Cons

While it is mostly a good thing, all the diversity, acceptance, and freedom in Playa del Carmen does come with a potential downside. Put simply, life in Mexico is not for everyone, and people need to have a certain character in order to live happily Playa del Carmen. You must be willing to change and be flexible.

Another negative aspect of the cultural diversity that dominates Playa del Carmen is the fact that animosity between the local Mexicans the foreigners does sometimes occur. The city is accepting for the most part, but be prepared to encounter certain divisions if you move there.

Cost of Housing: Pros

For the most part, the cost of living in Playa is lower than in the US. Although Playa del Carmen is more expensive than other parts of Mexico, it is more affordable than almost any coastal city in America. It is also cheaper than Cancun. If you want to live on the beach without spending too much, then Playa del Carmen is a good choice.

The recent surge in the expat population has caused rental and real estate prices to increase somewhat in Playa. The city is loved by tourists, expats, and investors, so housing is not as cheap as it used to be, but it is still pleasantly affordable.

If you want to maintain a home in Playa that is similar to what you would expect in the US, then be prepared to pay about $700-$1,000 per month for a furnished 3-bedroom condo. The average price for a luxury 3-bedroom home with a pool is about $1,500 per month.

Cost of Housing: Cons

Beachfront property is expensive, whether you rent or buy. Like anywhere else, the closer you get to the beach, the more you should expect to pay. Oceanfront property is expensive, and if you want to live right on the beach, you're going to pay a lot more.

Buying real estate is more difficult in Mexico, unless you have the ability to buy with cash. People don't usually finance a home here, the way they do in the United States. It's much less common.

If you're thinking of buying real estate in Playa del Carmen, prices range from $85,000 for a small home to over $2,000,000 for a spacious oceanfront hacienda. You can purchase a nice condo starting at about $100,000. Also, while mortgages are available, interest rates in the area are prohibitive for many, and most owners in Playa del Carmen prefer cash deals or private financing.

Tip! If you decide to buy a home or land in Playa del Carmen, always work with trusted real estate companies. There are real estate scammers everywhere, including Mexico, so exercise caution!

If you have children, don't forget to budget for the cost of their tuition when you are choosing housing. While prices vary from school to school, plan to spend about $400 per month on each child's education. Public schools are free, but most expats choose to send their children to private schools.

Employment: Pros

Playa del Carmen is developing quickly, which means that there are many more employment opportunities there than there used to be. Many expats work in hotels, restaurants, or bars, but many others decide to open a business in Playa del Carmen. Playa also offers jobs in travel, education, marketing, sales, and medicine. While the amount of jobs that are available varies with the season, there are usually a wide variety of options to choose from.

Employment: Cons

You cannot work in Mexico unless you apply for some type of permanent residency, which means a visitor's visa isn't enough.

Moving and Living on a Budget

Everyone is naturally concerned with their future and financial security, and not everyone has the funds they need to retire comfortably in the US. This is one of the reasons that Mexico is so tempting—it offers people the chance to retire and to live comfortably on a budget.

It's true that Playa is developing and attracting more and more expats and that prices rise with such increases in growth and popularity, but the cost of living in Playa continues to be lower than in the US. In fact, living along the Riviera Maya costs about 40% less than living in the US, Canada, or Europe.

Moving on a Budget

Keeping your expenses to the minimum from the moment you decide to move to the actual moving day takes effort but will pay off in the long run.

Selling most of your personal belongings that are replaceable or that you don't need will help you cover some of your moving expenses. Another way to keep moving expenses to a minimum is to find a home or apartment in Playa that is already furnished and to then sell the furniture that you already own. Moving and storing large items can be costly, so keep that in mind when planning your move.

Tip! When searching for an apartment in Playa del Carmen, you should try to contact local apartment owners in person. You can even wander the streets and call the phone numbers on every "For Rent" (Se Renta) sign you pass. The best deals are found on foot in this region. You can save a lot of money by searching this way, since many properties are not listed online and those that are tend to be more expensive than those that aren't.

Living on a Budget

US and Canadian dollars are valuable in Mexico (1 US dollar is currently worth about 13 pesos), which helps expats spend less on food, beverages, household supplies, transportation, and real estate in Playa than they would in their home country.

When it comes to long-term financial stability, expats have little to worry about, since the Mexican economy is among the top 14 economies in the world. Furthermore, most goods and services simply cost less in Mexico. Expats can often enjoy certain luxuries (like maid service) that they could never afford back in the US. Being able to afford maids, gardeners, nannies, and other luxuries means having more time to relax and to make the most of your time in Playa.

Health Care Costs in Mexico

Health care is always an issue when someone decides to expatriate. Fortunately, Mexican health care is relatively inexpensive, is easy to obtain, and is also of excellent quality. On top of that, medical care and prescription drugs in Mexico cost only a fraction of what they do in the US.

A private Mexican insurance policy for a family of 5 costs about $3,600 per year and offers worldwide coverage. If you decide that you only need to be covered in Mexico, then your costs will be reduced even further.

Planning for health care doesn't have to be difficult, but it can be more or less complicated depending on your individual situation and needs. For instance, those planning to retire in Playa can't count on their Medicare insurance, since Medicare does not offer coverage in Mexico.

US Medicare—Should I Keep It?

If you're planning to live indefinitely in Mexico but also want to travel back to the US frequently, you may want to purchase a Mexican policy while also keeping your US Medicare plan.

You can also choose to keep Medicare and just use local Mexican doctors as needed, but you will pay out of pocket. This is actually what most expat retirees do in Mexico. Instead of purchasing Mexican health care, they use Medicare as a backup, which they can use in the US for more serious health issues. This decision is motivated by the fact that health care in Mexico is significantly cheaper than in the US, and visiting a general practitioner is easy to do without spending much money.

Some expats have a pre-existing private insurance plan that provides coverage in Mexico, but most private insurance plans in the US don't. Before determining whether you need to switch your coverage, check your existing policy carefully to see if it will cover you while you are in Mexico. You should also figure out which documents you need to provide for your insurance company to cover any expenses incurred while abroad.

Health Care Options for Expats

Depending on your age, income, and health status, you can choose 1 or more of the following options to make sure your health care coverage is right for you:

- **Self-Insurance:** You can choose to pay for medical expenses out of pocket if you move to Mexico. Although this is not a practical course of action in the US, the low cost of healthcare in Mexico means that insurance is not necessary for everyone. If you don't have any health issues, you might pay less for routine tests and office visits by paying out of pocket than you would pay for ordinary insurance.
- **Private Insurance in Mexico:** Paying for private insurance in Mexico is a smart decision for many expats; especially since major medical and hospitalization insurance is much cheaper in Mexico than it is in the US.
- **Seguro Popular (Universal Health Care):** This is a government-funded program that is available to anyone in Mexico who chooses to enroll. This program was originally launched as a solution for the millions of Mexicans previously excluded from insurance and is often used by those with lower incomes.

Foreigners living in Mexico can benefit from free Social Security if they have a permanent or temporary residence visa. Foreigners that have only a visitor's visa can purchase IMSS health insurance privately if they choose.

Mexicans tend to prefer private health care to the state-run system, and most people who can afford to see a doctor in a private clinic opt for this solution. Usually, private health care means shorter waiting times and better service.

Most low-income Mexicans don't purchase private health insurance; instead, they use medical clinics since they are so affordable. The fee for a general consultation can be as low as $20.

Private hospitals in Guadalajara, Monterrey, and Mexico City offer some of the most advanced care centers in the world. The doctors in these world-class hospitals are experts in a variety of fields, including cardiovascular surgery, neurological surgery, orthopedic surgery, and organ transplants, and many have trained in the US and Europe.

Tip! Most private hospitals don't accept foreign health insurance and require cash or credit payment prior to admission or treatment. However, if a patient is seriously injured or is in particularly bad health, they will first attempt to stabilize their condition before transferring them to a government hospital.

Emergency Medical Evacuation Policies

If you are someone who likes to prepare for the worst, then you may want to purchase a policy that covers medical evacuation. There are many companies that specialize in providing emergency medical evacuation; those described below are currently the most popular in Mexico.

- **Global Underwriters** (globalunderwriters.com) has several policies that include coverage in Mexico. This company offers emergency evacuation services, as well as repatriation services for the remains of a loved one.

- **SkyMed** (skymed.com) has a policy designed especially for expats, which provides dual coverage and assures transportation from your home or hospital in Mexico to the US for medical reasons. The policy also includes transportation to Mexico from any areas where you have been hospitalized and are covered by your policy. The company offers coverage in Mexico, the US, Canada, the Caribbean, Belize, and Costa Rica.

Entertainment Costs

Entertainment costs include eating out, partying in local clubs, and visiting the tourist attractions in the area. Going to the cinema and playing (or watching) certain sports are also available options. Festivals and parades (which are usually free to attend) are another great way to have fun.

Nightlife is exciting in Playa del Carmen, and the city has plenty of clubs and beach bars to enjoy in the evenings. The city also has a number of flamenco bars and more traditional restaurants, where you can unwind and enjoy a drink while listening to live mariachi music.

Alcohol can be expensive in the beach clubs, and cover charges vary a lot based on the time of year and the popularity of the club.

Transportation

Transportation is cheap in Playa del Carmen, and you can easily get to just about any place in the city on foot or by bike. You don't need a bus or taxi to get anywhere, which is good for saving money and also makes it easier for residents to stay fit. Apartments are usually located within walking distance of stores, restaurants, and the beach.

If you ever do need a taxi, they can be found anywhere and are quite cheap. Prices start at $2 and are based on kilometers driven. And you can always get an estimate from the driver before you hop into the car so there aren't any surprises.

If you prefer to use public transportation, you can use local buses and shuttles for just a few pesos.

If you are living in Playa, you can get to pretty much anywhere in town on foot or by bicycle. That being said, there are a number of transportation options that make it easy to get around this beautiful city.

Buses are mostly used to get to other towns along the Riviera Maya and to the various attractions in the area. The bus system in Mexico is reliable and cheap. First class buses go to just about any destination in Mexico. First Class buses are luxurious vehicles and come with toilets and television service. They also have reserved seats and baggage check.

Second and third class buses run on set daily routes. Local buses (Mayab buses) are modern and comfortable, but they make more stops and are much cheaper.

There are also several bus lines that run up and down Highway 307. Buses coming from Cancun and Tulum stop at the Riviera (Playa) bus station, at the corner of Avenue Juarez and 5th Avenue. Buses coming from destinations in the interior of peninsula or out of state arrive at the ADO station on Avenida 20 between 12th and 14th streets.

Colectivos are small shuttles that provide services up and down Highway 307, connecting Playa del Carmen to Tulum and Cancun. You can catch the colectivo in Playa del Carmen at Calle 2 Norte between 15th and 20th Avenue (a 5-minute walk from 5th Avenue) and along Highway 307.

Note! You can wait for a colectivo anywhere along the highway in Playa. If a colectivo flashes its headlights when approaching you, it means it has space for you and will stop. It's also a good idea to wave your arm as it approaches to make sure that the driver knows to stop.

Colectivos run from Playa del Carmen to Cancun and Tulum on a daily basis (every 5-15 minutes from 5 am to 10 pm). Colectivos have air conditioning and allow luggage transportation.

Tip! Avoid traveling by colectivo during the peak hours, especially around 5 pm, because they can get very crowded. Sometimes a Mayab bus will stop when you're waiting for a colectivo. If it does, don't hesitate to jump on board; the cost is the same, and the bus will stop at the 5th Avenue terminal in Playa del Carmen.

Always be on the lookout for your stop. Even if you've told the driver where you want to get off, he may not remember by the time he reaches your destination. Payment is made when you exit the colectivo. There is no fixed schedule for colectivos, since they usually wait to be filled before departure.

Playa del Carmen also has several car rental companies. Most of the rental agencies available in town can also be found at the Cancun International Airport. The rates are usually lower when you rent directly at the airport, so keep that in mind when you are travelling.

Note! Consider purchasing a Mexican auto insurance policy and don't count on the auto insurance offered by your credit card because it might not cover driving in Mexico. Verify your coverage before you rent. The insurance coverage should include an attorney and claims adjusters, which will come to the scene of any accidents that may occur.

If you do rent a car at the airport, it's not uncommon for the rental car companies to initiate a "hard sell" for insurance, upgrades, and even timeshares. Just decline anything that you don't feel comfortable with.

Don't let the salespeople pressure you into purchasing things that you don't need.

You don't need a car to live in Playa, but if you are planning to buy one there, here are some tips:

- **Choose a white car.** White cars reflect the sun better than darker colors, which helps keep them cooler on Playa's hot and sunny days.

- **Choose a car that has decent ground clearance.** Like many cities in Mexico, Playa has a lot of speed bumps, which are meant to help slow traffic down. A car with bad suspension, a low front spoiler, or low ground clearance is not well-suited to Playa's roads.

- **Seriously consider buying a new car.** Buying a used car in Mexico is a risky business, because Mexicans tend to use their cars until they are almost entirely worn out. Unless you are knowledgeable about car repair yourself, you might find yourself taking the same clunker to the repair shop again and again.

Buying Other Goods in Playa

Though many things are affordable in Playa (like food), brand-name clothing and many electronics are not. You can expect to pay more for Nike shoes in Mexico than you would in the US.

Because most of these items have to be imported, they usually cost more in Mexico than they do in the US. However, you still can find plenty of deals and bargains if you know how to shop like locals do.

Some expats choose to buy fabric and make their own clothes (and even some interior design elements, like curtains). Plenty of stores in Playa del Carmen sell everything a person could need to expand their wardrobe and decorate their home while saving money. Many stores also offer the services of local seamstresses, who can create custom designs for you at a low rate. Remember, labor is cheap in Mexico, so you might find that a tailored wardrobe is within your budget there.

You can also look for bargains at yard sales, too. There are "garage sales" in Playa del Carmen, just like anywhere else. A great place to find used furniture, clothing, kitchen items, and even used cars is to search through the local papers and find families that are moving back to the US. They rarely take their household back with them, and you can find many bargains that way.

Save Money by Living like a Local

As with any other city, the cost of living in Playa doesn't end with housing, utilities, food, and entertainment.

Generally speaking, a couple should budget some money for recurring monthly expenses in Playa. This includes money for food and housing, but will vary depending on an individual's preferences and hobbies. If you decide to limit the nights you spend in town or don't plan to take many day trips, you could enjoy life in Playa with a partner for about $700 per month. We know this is possible because the local Mexicans usually survive on much less.

It's good to know that the average Mexican family of 4 manages to live on only $400 a month in Playa del Carmen. The low cost of living in Mexico paired with the fact that many Mexicans choose to live a frugal life helps them to keep costs down.

If you want to save money, then consider living like a middle-class Mexican family would. Shop at neighborhood markets like the locals do, shop for deals (even if that means going to more than one store), and avoid making extravagant purchases.

Do You Have Passive Income?

Most expats who come to Playa del Carmen aren't looking to secure a new job or to start a business. Instead, many work remotely as copywriters, travel writers, bloggers, and IT workers. Still, many others count on passive sources of income such as Social Security or money from rental properties they own back in the US.

According to the US State Department, 1 million American citizens of all ages live in Mexico, and this number continues to grow. One reason for this trend is the fact that the same Social Security that might cover only the cost of utilities in the US can buy someone a very comfortable life in Mexico.

The average Social Security check is about $1,200, which is more than enough for two people to live in Playa, if one lives frugally. When paired with additional sources of income, Social Security makes it possible for many expats to live quite lavishly, (especially compared to most Mexican families, who are accustomed to living on much less).

Expats from the US can receive Social Security while living in Mexico as long as they remain eligible. The US periodically sends out questionnaires, which you will have to fill out and return if you want to continue receiving benefits. Make sure to fill out such questionnaires quickly, completely, and honestly to avoid penalties.

If you move to Playa, you may want to have your Social Security payment deposited directly into your account at a financial institution in the US. You can then withdraw the funds yourself or can transfer them to an account you hold in Mexico. This alternative will help you avoid check-cashing and currency-conversion fees.

Working Online to Support Yourself

Working remotely over the internet is one of the most popular methods of earning money among expats in Playa. Working this way allows people to work from the comfort of their own home, to make their own schedule, and to enjoy enough flexibility to truly enjoy their life in Playa.

With the rapid development of the internet, more and more businesses are choosing to hire people online. Working online is a great way to earn money while freeing yourself from the more rigid schedule of a traditional job. Today's businesses are more portable and more digital than ever, and modern communication technologies present people with many more long-distance working opportunities than they used to have.

The most popular fields among those who work online are copywriting, IT, web design, photography, travel writing, and online businesses that can be run from all over the world. People are becoming more and more creative when it comes to finding ways to make money online, and it really is possible to enjoy a good life in Playa while working solely on your own computer in your own home.

Playa del Carmen also provides everything a person could need to make sure that their online business flourishes. Mexico has the best and most developed telecommunications network in Latin America. You will easily be able to find high speed data connections, Wi-Fi, and mobile internet in Playa, and you will also be able to access such services for a reasonable price.

Taxes for Expats

If you are an American Citizen or Legal US Resident (green card holder), you are required to file a US Income Tax Return, even if you live and work abroad.

The US has income tax treaties with over 42 countries (including Mexico), which enable the IRS and foreign tax authorities to exchange information pertaining to their citizens who live in the other country. These treaties reduce or eliminate any double taxation of your income by both countries by allowing credits for foreign income taxes you pay while living outside the US. However, such credits are not automatic, and you need to file a US return in order to claim them.

If you fail to file your tax return, remember that there is no statute of limitations on tax assessments. The longer you take to pay what you owe, the worse your situation will become.

Interview with IJ Zemelman, EA

IJ Zemelman is a licensed enrolled agent and the president of *Taxes for Expats*, a professional firm that specializes in the preparation of tax returns for expats all around the world.

Q: To begin, why don't you tell us a little bit about your firm?

IJ: Thank you very much for the invite to chat! We've been preparing expatriate tax returns for 24 years and have clients in over 150 countries.

Q: There's a lot of misinformation out there about how expats are taxed and what their filing requirements are. What are some of the most common questions that you receive from potential clients?

These are the most common questions we receive:

1. Do I have to file if I live abroad and have no US income?
2. Will I have to pay tax to the IRS on my foreign income?

3. What if I don't file? Will the government find me and what consequences will I face?
4. Does my non-American spouse have to report their income?
5. Can I get a refund?

The answers to these questions can be complex, and they vary from person to person. Every expat's situation is unique.

Q: Can you talk a little more about your clients? What are they like? Where are they from?

IJ: Over the years, we have filed US expat returns for every job imaginable, and at last count, we had served clients in 152 different countries.

In recent years, our client base has broadened from expats to "accidental" American citizens as well. Which is to say that we serve a number of people who may have never stepped foot inside the US but are still citizens—either because of their parents, or because they left the US at a young age.

Now, with increased focus on FATCA, (the Foreign Account Tax Compliance Act) many expats are being contacted by their local banks or (in a better scenario) they are being proactive and reading about their requirement to file and are coming to us to get back into compliance.

Over the past several years, the IRS has introduced some great programs such as the Streamlined Procedure, which allows for penalty forgiveness and a clean slate in exchange for an agreement to continue filing from here on out. Many expats have taken advantage of these programs in order to get a "fresh start."

Q: Do you have any specific advice for American expats who have decided to live in Mexico?

IJ: A point to consider is that Mexico, like the United States, taxes their residents on their worldwide income. It is also important to note that

Mexico allows for a foreign tax credit for any taxes paid outside of Mexico. So does the United States. As a result, a taxpayer may be required to pay taxes in *both* countries, but will also have offsetting tax credits. Also, since the US has a foreign earned income exclusion of approximately $100K per person ($200K per married couple); having to pay US income tax may never come into play for many expats.

Q: What about dual citizens? If an expat has both US and Mexican citizenship, how does that affect their tax situation?

IJ: The IRS stance on any other citizenship you may hold is very simple— they don't care. Your obligations with respect to filing US taxes are exactly the same, regardless of whether or not you have Mexican citizenship.

Q: What if I have a bank account in Mexico? Does that require any additional tax filings?

IJ: If you have over $10,000 in a Mexican bank (or in *any* bank outside the US) at *any* point during the year, then you have to file a special form called a Foreign Bank Account Report (FBAR). It was created specifically for the purpose of reporting non-US financial accounts to the US Treasury.

Q: What if I live and work in Mexico and pay taxes in Mexico? Do I have to pay taxes to the US too? Can I exclude any of my earnings?

IJ: You probably won't have to pay any US taxes. As I mentioned, the first $100k or so should be tax-free, and you can also deduct any income taxes you pay in Mexico from your US tax obligation. So, most people don't have to pay anything to the IRS when they live in Mexico in the end. Moreover, certain types of income have lower tax rates in the United States than in Mexico. For instance, there is a 15% tax on capital gains in the US, but the Mexican tax rate on capital gains may be as high as 30%. As a result, the tax credit from any tax paid on capital gains in Mexico will fully offset the capital gain tax in the US.

Q: What happens if I own a home or a rental property in Mexico? Do I have to report anything?

IJ: Prior to June 2013, US taxpayers with Mexican property *fideicomisos* were required to file foreign trust return forms 3520 and 3520-A, which was a burdensome and expensive annual exercise. In June 2013, the IRS made a final ruling that a Mexican Land Trust no longer needs to file as foreign trusts as long as the real estate trust holds just *one* property and only allows just *one* activity (namely, "holding title to the property").

If these conditions are met, a Mexican Land Trust is not considered a Foreign Trust according to the IRS filing requirements for foreign trusts. This is true whether or not the property is rented out.

By the same token, the value of the *fideicomiso* is not included in valuation of your foreign financial assets and is not required to be reported on FBAR or FATCA forms.

Q: Do you have any other advice for someone who is considering a permanent move to Mexico?

IJ: One thing people sometimes forget to consider are the requirements a foreign resident must satisfy in order to obtain a homestead exemption on the sale of their principal residence in Mexico.

If the homeowner has only one home, and is that home is in Mexico, then they should be able to get a homestead exemption. However, if they have a home in Mexico and another in the US, it may be difficult to get an exemption, especially if the homeowner's income is not derived from Mexican sources.

Q: Thanks for all the great advice! How can we contact you if we have a tax-related question?

IJ: Our website is *www.taxesforexpats.com*. Anyone with questions should feel free to contact us at any time—we are always happy to help!

Essential Steps Before You Leave

Whatever their reasons for expatriating and regardless of their final destination, there are certain steps that all 6.6 million of the US citizens who move abroad each year must take. Moving to a new country isn't something one does overnight. Expatriation takes time and careful planning.

3 Months Before Departure

Passport and Visa

3 months before you plan to move, you should already have a valid passport and should have applied for a visa that will allow you to visit Mexico. In order to apply for a visa, your passport will need to be valid for at least 1 year into the future; if your passport does not meet this requirement, make sure to renew it as soon as you decide to expatriate. If you plan to stay in Mexico for longer than 6 months, you may also want to apply for permanent residency. If you're planning on moving permanently, consider hiring an immigration attorney to help you with all the paperwork.

Get Your House in Order—Literally

If you own real estate, you will need to decide what you want to do with it before you move. Keeping it (and paying taxes on it), renting it, and selling it are all options. Your decision will depend on your individual needs as well as the type of property you own.

If you are planning to sell your house, it should already be on the market 3 months from your departure date.

If you're living in a rented accommodation, make sure to check the details of your lease before you plan your move.

> **Tip!** If you plan on moving to Mexico permanently, don't sell your house or end your current lease until your permanent residency is confirmed.

Consider Your Vehicles

Before moving, make sure you have plans for any cars, trucks, boats or other vehicles you own. It costs a good deal of money to move such vehicles from the US to Mexico, so if you choose to sell them, make sure that you service them and put them on the market well before your departure date.

Temporary Accommodation in Playa

If you're not planning to move straight into a permanent home in Playa del Carmen, make sure to book any temporary accommodations you might need well in advance. This is especially important if you're planning to move during the high seasons (Christmas, Easter, and summer). It's almost impossible to get a room on short notice when all the tourists are in town.

If you are planning to buy a home in Mexico, you should count on having temporary accommodation for at least a few weeks (and possibly for a few months). Finalizing the sale on a house doesn't happen overnight.

Electrical Appliances

Voltages in Mexico are the same as in the US, so the electrical devices that you already own will work just fine in Playa. However, while it's practical to bring small devices like laptops and cell phones, paying to move larger appliances may not make sense financially. Before you choose which appliances to bring with you, look into the costs of moving them and compare those numbers to the costs of buying them new in Mexico.

Pets

If you want to take your pets to Mexico, you will need to apply for permission at your local Mexican Consulate. Make sure that all your pet's papers are in order. You will need a Health Certificate issued by an official authority or a licensed veterinarian and proof that vaccines against rabies and distemper were administrated at least 15 days before your arrival in Mexico.

While cats and dogs don't need additional special permits to be taken to Mexico, other pets like birds and snakes might require them.

If you don't want to take your pets with you, start searching for an alternative home for them well before the day on which you plan to move.

What Stays and What Goes?

Tip! *Keep only the essentials. De-clutter your life! The more you get rid of, the easier your move will be.*

Make a list of all your possessions and determine which items are essential and which are not. Once you know what you won't be taking with you, you will also need to determine whether you want to store, sell, or give away those items. Also, keep in mind that you have to have a residence visa in order to take large amounts of household items and furniture into Mexico; simple tourists are not allowed to bring such items with them.

There are plenty of moving companies that provide door-to-door services, so it's not that difficult to get all of your personal items moved to your home in Mexico once you're settled in.

You should also consider renting a furnished home in Playa, which will further reduce the list of items you need to worry about bringing with you.

2 Months Before Departure

Contact Moving Companies

As your departure date gets closer, take some time to get quotes from moving companies. By this point, you should know what you will be taking with you, which will help you get more exact quotes and will determine the exact type of transportation that you will need. Do your research and choose a moving company that has a great reputation. You get what you pay for, and you don't want to take unnecessary risks with your belongings.

Make Sure Everything is Ready for Your Arrival

You will probably arrive in Mexico ahead of your belongings, but you still need to make sure that you have a place to keep them while you look for permanent housing. Securing a permanent residence could take a while, so you may need to look into renting storage in Mexico for a while.

> **Note!** You are only allowed to import certain items duty-free if you have a residence visa and if you are able to present a list (called a "*Menaje de Casa*") of your items at the border; but some personal items (like clothes and books) are allowed duty-free regardless. Taxes need to be paid for electrical goods and home appliances that exceed the duty limit, which is another reason it's a good idea to bring only the essentials. If you are unsure about anything, get in touch with a moving company that can help you with all the rules and paperwork.

Arranging for Your Children's' Education

Make any arrangements for your children's schooling at least 6 weeks before moving. If you are moving to Playa for a job, then the cost of schooling may be included in the relocation package provided by the company you work for, but if you're moving on your own, you will need to carefully research schools and plan your budget accordingly. As a foreigner, you should probably limit your search to private schools in Playa that offer bilingual or trilingual education.

Book Your Plane Tickets

If you are flying to Playa del Carmen, make sure to make your airline reservation in advance to get the best deal. Most travelers flying to

Playa land at Cancun International Airport, which is located about 45 minutes away. Cozumel International airport is another great option (and is actually closer to Playa than Cancun). Playa del Carmen does have a small airport, but it is served mostly by small flights to Cozumel, Chichén Itzá, and Palenque.

If you will be travelling with pets, make sure to follow the airline's rules and regulations for bringing animals with you to Mexico.

Take Care of Your Documents and Financial Arrangements

Don't start selling your belongings or make any moving or travel arrangements if you don't have your visa confirmed. Make sure that all of your travel documents are in order. You should also take a moment to locate and organize your birth certificates, marriage certificates, diplomas, and other personal papers.

Once your documents are in order, close any credit cards or bank accounts you won't be using while in Mexico. Of course, you can also choose to keep your current accounts open. Due to the widespread availability of online banking, direct deposit, and ATMs, many expats continue banking in the US while living in Mexico.

Tip! Make sure to shred any documents containing personal and financial details to avoid identity theft. It's harder to deal with identity theft outside the country.

If you are going to move to Playa, consider having at least 2 primary financial accounts: 1 in the US and 1 Mexico. You will then have the option of using the US account to access cash and payments (like Social Security) in your home currency and to pay any financial obligations that you have back in your home country (such as mortgages, loans, and tax payments).

Make sure to establish any accounts you want to have in the US before your departure, since it's nearly impossible to open a bank account in the US with a foreign address.

> **Tip!** Work with well-established and nationally available banks. Larger US banks, (like Wells Fargo, Chase, and Bank of America) are better choices than smaller banks if you expatriate. These banks typically allow users to do most of their banking online, and they often offer better exchange rates and faster international wire transfers. Many of the larger banks offer 24-hour banking as well.

For everyday financial needs, you will eventually need to have a bank account in Playa. Having a Mexican bank account will make it easier for you to pay for any unexpected costs without having to wire transfer your money from the US to Mexico, which often involves added fees.

Financial Documents and Taxes

If you're still a US citizen while living in Mexico and you have more than $10,000 in your new accounts, you will need to file a Report of Foreign Bank and Financial Accounts (FBAR) with the IRS. There is no limit on the amount of money that you can import to or export from Mexico, but if the amount is over, $10,000, you need to declare it.

If you are wealthy enough to need to fill out an FBAR and don't want to do the necessary paperwork, your only other option is to renounce your US citizenship. Don't make this decision in a hurry and don't close all your US savings, checking, and credit accounts unless you are absolutely sure that you won't be moving back to the US.

If you plan to rent a house in Playa del Carmen, you will need to have all your pension and investment papers in order, because the Mexican authorities may ask for proof of your income. If you are employed or have your own business, you should be prepared to present bank statements and recent pay stubs.

Find a Financial Advisor with Expat Experience

Expatriating is much easier if you consult a financial advisor with cross-border expertise. A good financial advisor can save you a lot of time and can help you choose where to hold your assets and how to manage your investment portfolio. They can also refer you to other professionals who will understand your unique situation as an expat.

This is especially important for American Citizens, because the IRS instituted new reporting requirements for foreign accounts. Being a United States citizen (or legal resident, a "green card holder") requires that you file a yearly tax return with the IRS, no matter where you live.

In addition to filing a tax return, many expats are also required to file an FBAR to report foreign assets and/or foreign bank accounts. The penalties for failing to file the FBAR are extremely harsh. Speak with a tax advisor about this issue before you expatriate, so you can understand your filing requirements *before* it's too late.

1 Month Before Departure
Verify Your Housing Arrangements

If you have a landlord in the US, verify that they are aware of your departure date. If you are selling your home, you should have already closed on the sale or should be close to doing so. If you are keeping your home, make sure you have arranged to have someone take care of the property. If you are renting your property, you should have already chosen tenants and should be making final preparations for their arrival.

Making Sure Everything is Sold, Stored, and Packed Properly

By now, you should have sold any belongings you are planning to sell and should have arranged storage for any items you want to keep but won't be bringing to Mexico.

Don't forget to carefully clear out every nook and cranny of your home. You may also need to dismantle any furniture that can't be transported as is.

Tip! Order plenty of boxes, tape, and bubble wrap ahead of time! Good packing supplies will help you pack quickly and effectively. Spend the extra money required to get sturdy boxes and good packaging, so that you don't have to worry about anything getting damaged in transit. You should also start packing as soon as possible to reduce the stress of moving.

Announce Your Move

Don't forget to let all your family, friends, and colleagues that you are moving to Mexico. You also need to inform local authorities, your property management association, utility services, the telephone and TV companies, and all your financial institutions of your moving plans. And don't forget to cancel any newspaper or magazine subscriptions as well as any local club or gym memberships. If you have children, arrange for their last day at school. You will also need to collect all school certificates or report cards that they might need.

Get Copies of Your Medical Records

Let all your doctors know that you are moving and get copies of all of your family's medical records. If you have any prescriptions, you will also need to get copies of them and to make arrangements to continue getting the drugs that you need in Mexico.

Tip! It's a good idea to schedule a last health physical, optometrist appointment, and dental checkup for the whole family before moving.

Confirm Your Travel Arrangements

Get confirmation from any companies whose services will be part of your move to Mexico. These include cleaners, movers, and rental agencies. If you're not taking your pets with you, make final preparations to transfer them to their new home. If you are bringing them with you to Mexico, make sure you have all the required paperwork in order as well as the correct kennel or carrying containers.

1 Week Before Departure
Prepare to Leave Your Home

If you didn't manage to sell everything that you are not planning to store or take with you, then this is the time to donate or recycle those items. You should also empty and defrost your freezer and donate any extra food that's still in your cupboards.

Sort and label all of your boxes to help moving day go as smoothly as possible. You should also do any last-minute laundry or dry-cleaning.

> **Tip!** It might be easier for you to arrange to spend the last few nights before your departure in a hotel or with family, especially if you no longer have beds to sleep on.

Pack Your Bags

Pack any bags that you will be carrying with you when you move. Make sure you pack enough clothes to last you until the rest of your personal belongings arrive in Mexico. If you are flying to Playa, make sure to check the airline's weight limits and to pack anything that is particularly valuable to you in your carry-on luggage.

Moving Day
Cleaning Up

If you are working with a professional cleaning crew, make sure that you are ready for them to arrive. If you are moving and cleaning yourself, make sure that your property is entirely emptied of your belongings.

Read the Meters

Take final readings from your gas, water, and electricity meters, so that you can approximate your final bills for the property. Make sure that your landline phone service, internet, and cable TV are cancelled as well.

Re-check your Travel Documents and Paperwork

Make sure that all of your travel documents and other important papers are in order and that you can easily access them. Re-check everything one last time. You should carry any important documents with you on your person, and should not ship them or put them in checked baggage.

Want to Retire in Mexico?

Retirement Income

The exact amount of income you need to retire in Mexico depends on your lifestyle expectations.

Mexican Immigration requires you to demonstrate a proven fixed income in order to obtain a retirement visa in Mexico, but your regular Social Security might satisfy that requirement quite easily.

In 2015, the income requirements for a retirement visa changed to $1,400 monthly. These numbers are always in flux. The best way to get the current requirements is to contact your local Mexican consulate. Consulates are located in most major US cities.

If you decide to use a professional to help you apply, expect to pay around $400-$500 if you use a broker or lawyer.

Health Care for Retirees

Good health care is widely available in Playa, but Mexico has no reciprocal health care agreements with any other countries. This means that if you have a health care plan in the US (including Medicare), it will not cover your health care costs or prescriptions while you are living in Mexico.

Luckily, health care policies are more affordable in Mexico than in the US, but health insurance is more expensive as you age. For example, a comprehensive medical insurance policy covering 60-69 year olds would average about $5,200 pesos per year (about $400 USD for a full year's coverage, which includes prescriptions).

Those who decide to retire in Playa del Carmen are usually pleasantly surprised by the high quality of medical treatment that they receive. Many Mexican hospitals and clinics are equipped with state-of-the-art equipment and offer the same level of comfort offered in the US for more reasonable prices. Cancun, which is located only 45 minutes away from Playa, has several world-class hospitals and is home to a large number of specialists.

Purchasing Real Estate as a Retiree

Most who decide to retire in Playa del Carmen dream of buying a house near the coast, and the city provides them with the chance to fulfill this dream. Playa also offers real estate in a number of gated communities, which are often within walking distance of the beach and include green spaces, parks, and bike trails. Furthermore, many condo complexes in the area include pools and gyms, which help expats relax and stay fit while in Playa.

With the notable exception of electricity, utility bills are usually lower in Mexico than in the US, and property taxes and maintenance costs are both very low.

An estimated 90 million North Americans will be retiring over the next 10 years, and many of them will choose to retire in Mexico. Prices for real estate in Mexico are still lower than in the US (on average).

Tip! If you want to move to Playa del Carmen permanently, always consider renting a house for at least a year before making any big real estate purchases. Renting will give you a chance to get to know the community and neighborhood before settling there for good.

Although the bank system in Mexico has improved considerably in the recent years and is much more customer-focused than before, charges and interest rates on borrowing in Mexico are still higher than in the US, and the conditions for keeping an account open are stricter than you might expect. Most property purchases in Mexico are made in cash, but it is possible (but tricky) to finance a home in Mexico with a US bank. While some US banks offers mortgages for homes purchased in Mexico, many others do not.

Extra Benefits for Retirees in Mexico

Retiree expats can take advantage of certain benefits in Mexico as long as they have a valid residence visa. If you're 60 years old or older, you can get a senior citizen card through Mexico's national senior citizens' organization, the INAPAM. This card provides discounts on a variety of goods and services, including medical care and devices, airline and bus tickets, entrance fees to museums and archaeological sites, and even property taxes.

Working in a Tourist Zone

Not all expats come to Playa del Carmen to live on their social security checks or to start their own business. Some of them come searching for a local job that will enable them to enjoy a tranquil life in Playa del Carmen without having to worry about daily expenses.

Once you begin your job search, it's not enough to just send your resume to the company that you want to work for. In Mexico, it's best if you actually visit employers in person. Many employers in the city prefer to meet with candidates so that they can better assess their skills, and most employers in Playa post their job listings on their own doors rather than on the internet.

If you're planning to get a job in Playa del Carmen, you will almost definitely need to speak Spanish. Unemployment in Mexico is relatively high, and finding employment can be challenging even for Mexicans who speak the local language fluently. That being said, you could cater your business to other tourists, and many expats do this quite successfully, while speaking only conversational Spanish.

You should also remember that expats in Mexico often receive salaries that are smaller than they would receive in their home countries for the same job. Furthermore, companies must prove that hired expats are not taking jobs that Mexican workers would be able to do, which limits the types of jobs that expats are typically hired for.

Expats who work in the tourism field usually search for jobs at resorts, spas, or water sports centers. Many also work as guides in real estate or teach English. You shouldn't expect to get rich working in Playa, but you can make enough to cover your expenses while immersing yourself in a new culture.

Requirements for Working in Mexico

To work in Mexico for an extended period of time, you need to have at least a temporary residency visa. The first step is to go to a Mexican Consulate. If you are outside Mexico and apply for a temporary residence visa, the Consulate will issue a special visa in your passport for entering Mexico within 6 months. You'll then need to go the Cancun INM office within 30 days of entering the country.

If you already have a job offer from a company in Mexico, ask them to send you a letter on company letterhead as an official offer of employment. Such a letter will allow you to go to a Mexican consulate in your country and request a temporary residence visa, a permanent residence visa with permission to engage in paid work activities.

Employment in Mexico

If you're planning to work in Playa del Carmen, then you'll need to know a few things about Mexican labor law. This law regulates labor relations, labor unions, and labor courts. The federal labor law contains everything you need to know about things like minimum wage, the length of the work week, work days, and overtime rules.

Minimum wage in Mexico varies from region to region. A table listing the different minimum wages in Mexico can be found at conasami.gob.mx (Use Google to translate the page to English if you can't read Spanish). The law determines a minimum daily wage for every category of services as well as a minimum salary for each category of work. It also determines a minimum increase after an annual salary review.

The standard work week in Mexico is 48 hours. This is how long employees can work without being paid overtime. Overtime hours are double the hourly rate, for up to 9 overtime hours. Hours worked over this amount are paid triple, as are any hours worked that fall on a holiday. Employees who work on Sunday receive a 25% bonus over their ordinary wages for that day.

The work day is usually from 8 am to 4 pm, Monday through Friday, but there is often a 2-hour siesta between 2 pm and 4 pm.

In the tourism industry, the work week also includes Saturdays. There are usually 3 work shifts in a Mexican work day: the day shift (8 hours), the night shift (7 hours), and the mixed shift (7 ½ hours).

Opening a Small Business in Mexico

Some expats choose to open their own small business and become self-employed. While the process of opening a business is not exactly easy, it can definitely be worth the effort.

If you're considering opening a small hotel, a real estate agency, a tour company, or any other business that you think will flourish in Playa del Carmen, then you need to take things one step at a time and make sure you respect all the legal requirements along the way.

Find the Right Sector

Before opening a business, you must decide what type of business you want to run and then formulate a realistic plan. To do so, you must determine whether the business you have in mind will work well in Playa and whether it is suitable for a foreigner to run.

The Mexican Constitution makes it very clear that some commercial activities are reserved for the government, while others are to be conducted exclusively by Mexicans citizens. The following activities are reserved solely for Mexican citizens:

- Broadcast television
- Ground transportation
- The distribution and sale of gasoline

If you decide to apply for Mexican citizenship, then all of these jobs will be available for you, as well.

Most expat businesses in Playa thrive in sectors such as tourism and real estate. Some expats open restaurants, bars, nightclubs, or retail stores that sell items that otherwise can't be found in Playa. There are many possibilities for starting a business in Playa. You just need to find the one that suits you and then do what it takes to make it happen.

Getting Started

Gathering all the legal documents and the paperwork you need to start your own business can be a time-consuming and stressful process. The good news is that Playa del Carmen is not a big city, so everywhere you will need to go for paperwork and licensing will be close by.

If you want to start your own business, you need get your legal documents in order first. You will also have to translate these documents into Spanish.

> **Note!** Most documents issued by foreign governments—including birth certificates, school records, professional degrees, marriage licenses, and divorce decrees—are not valid for use in Mexico until they receive a special certification from your home government (in the US, this is called an "apostille" and is issued by your Secretary of State. In California, for example, an apostille costs about $20 per document). Once the documents are approved for use in Mexico, such documents will need to be translated by a translator authorized by the Mexican government.

Before opening a business in Mexico, you need to carefully consider how long you plan to stay there. If you don't want to stay in Playa forever but choose to open a business, you will need an exit plan. You also need to consider the fact that it's almost impossible to sell a Mexican business or Mexican real estate while you are living abroad. If you want to return to your home country and decide to sell your business at a later date, you will need to remain in Mexico long enough to sign documents, promote the sale of your business, etc. Opening a business in a foreign country is a decision that has long-term consequences and that should not be taken lightly.

> **Tip:** Don't start a business in Playa that you wouldn't start at home, and don't start one that you don't know anything about.

Profits Depend on the Season

Playa del Carmen is a tourist destination, and many businesses that flourish during tourist season stagnate during the rest of the year. You need to know how to budget and stretch your dollars during the off season, otherwise your business may fail quickly.

April and May are considered slower months. Hurricane season lasts from June to September, so you also have to be prepared for that. The busy season starts in December and runs through January. People who wish to visit Playa Del Carmen during this time usually have to book at least six months in advance.

Even popular businesses in Playa often shut their doors during at least part of the low season, because it is simply not profitable enough to leave them open. If your business depends on tourists, you will need to make enough during the high season to support your business for the entire year.

More Money-Making Ideas for Expats

If you find that the work opportunities mentioned above are not really what you're searching for, you could also consider getting a job as a timeshare seller. This is a pretty common job for expats in Playa, (because of their language skills) but it requires strong sales skills and the right employer.

If you don't want to form a business in Playa del Carmen from scratch, buying an already-established business is also an option. Small hotels, restaurants, and apartment buildings are the most common types of businesses available for sale. You can work with a broker to find a business that is right for you. If you want to purchase an existing business in Playa, you need to have cash to invest.

There are many things you can do to make money in Playa del Carmen. What is most important is to make sure that you work legally and that all your documents are in order. You wouldn't want to lose your right to live in paradise just because you forgot to sign a paper! And remember to pay your taxes in the US, especially if you're working as a freelancer or have your own business online. No matter what your job, it's best to hire professional advisors, who will make sure that you work in accordance with both the American and Mexican laws.

Visas and Residency: Basic Info

There are multiple visas that allow a foreign national to visit and stay in Mexico. After one obtains a permanent resident visa, he or she can apply for Mexican citizenship after waiting for a period of time.

While most visitors can easily obtain a visitor's visa, citizens from certain countries need to request an Entry Permit before arriving at the border. This extra requirement does not apply to citizens of the US, Canada, or countries in the European Union.

Exactly which type of visa you need depends mostly on why you are visiting Playa del Carmen and on how long you plan to stay there. You can buy real estate in Playa del Carmen if you have a visitor visa, a temporary residence visa, or a permanent residence visa.

Which Mexican Visa is Right for Me?

Just want to explore a little bit? A visitor's visa is the simplest option if you're planning to stay in Mexico for less than 180 days (approximately 6 months). This gives you plenty of time to visit the area and explore. A visitor's visa does not give you the right to work.

Want to stay longer than 6 months? A temporary residence visa is the best choice if you're planning to stay for between 180 days and 4 years and plan to travel back to the US on a regular basis.

Ready to expatriate for good? Apply for a permanent residence visa if you're planning to stay in Mexico permanently.

If you need to be able to work in Playa and already have a job offer from a Mexican company, then you only need to get a temporary residence visa to begin with. The company you work for will sponsor you and obtain a work visa for you on your behalf.

A permanent residence visa will allow you to apply for a job in Mexico (as long as the job is not one that is reserved exclusively for Mexican citizens).

Mexican law establishes three migratory categories for the stay of foreigners in Mexico:

- Visitor
- Temporary Resident
- Permanent Resident

We'll discuss the differences between these three visas next.

The Easy Visa: a Visitor's Visa

If you live in the US, Canada, or the European Union, you don't need to apply for a visitor's visa before your arrival to Mexico. These countries are on Mexico's "no visa required list," and people from them do not have to formally apply for a visa at a Mexican consulate. When you arrive in Mexico, you will be given a tourist visa at the airport. Tourists pay about $22 for a visitor visa, which allows them to stay in Mexico for 180 days.

Airlines usually collect the visa fee on behalf of the Mexican government by including it in the cost of airfare. If you don't arrive in Mexico by plane, you will pay the fee separately at the immigration check-point when you cross.

If you lose your visitor visa, you will be required to apply for a replacement before you leave. A replacement costs about $45 and takes about a day to receive.

If you overstay the limit on your visitor visa, you will have to visit an immigration office and pay a fine before you can leave Mexico. The exact amount of the fine is determined on a per-day basis, but it tends to be rather expensive.

It's important to keep your visa safe. If you do not have it with you when you leave the country, you will encounter some red tape and be forced to pay for an exit permit. Losing your visa causes unpleasant delays and may cause you to miss your flight.

Tip! If you are traveling on a cruise ship and dock at a Mexican port, you don't need a visitor visa to enter the country. Special arrangements are made for passengers who visit Mexico temporarily while on cruises.

Some expats who don't plan to work in Playa extend their visitor visa by crossing the border when it expires, only to return and ask for a new one that will allow them to spend another 180 days in Mexico. Some expats will do this for years, and there are even bus services that cater to them. Most of the time, expats will drive into Belize, stay for a day or two, and then cross back into Mexico after renewing their visa.

This gets tiresome after a while, so if you are planning to stay in Mexico for more than 180 days, the best thing to do is apply for a temporary or permanent residence visa.

Temporary and Permanent Resident Visas

After a visitor's visa, the next step is to apply for a Temporary Residence Visa or a Permanent Residence Visa. Both will allow you to stay and work in the country, but there are some major differences between the two.

A Temporary Resident Visa has lower income requirements than a Permanent Residence Visa. A Temporary Residence Visa is mainly designed for people who want to live in Mexico for an extended period of time, and who also want to work in the country. A Temporary Visa will allow you to remain in the country for up to four years. After 4 years it can be converted to a Permanent Resident Visa. You will need to show proof of income in order to apply for this visa, unless you qualify for the visa another way (marriage to a Mexican citizen is another way to obtain this visa).

A Permanent Resident Visa leads up to Mexican citizenship, which is optional. Once you apply and receive permanent residency, you can remain a permanent resident as long as you like. Unlike a Temporary Residence Visa, this visa does not have to be renewed.

Ready to Take the Final Plunge? Applying for Mexican Citizenship

There some expats who decide to stay in Mexico for good. If you're planning to stay in Playa forever and want to enjoy all the rights and privileges that come with Mexican citizenship, then naturalization might be the right path for you.

You have to ask yourself—is Mexican citizenship *worth it* for me? Becoming a Mexican citizen is not easy and takes time. But it also confers a lot of benefits. Becoming a citizen will prevent you from waiting in long immigration lines at the airport and will enable you to enjoy easier processes in banking and legal matters. Citizenship also grants the right to vote, and a Mexican voter registration card is a better form of identification to have than a passport when cashing checks or dealing with government agencies.

Since citizens have priority in the Mexican job market, citizenship will increase your job prospects and will allow you to apply for jobs in a wider range of fields. Citizens can also own land in their name without having to pay for a fideicomiso, so if you would like to own coastal property, and you have your heart set on an oceanfront home in Playa, then applying for Mexican citizenship might be a good idea.

Hiring an immigration lawyer is a good way to make sure that the process goes as smoothly as possible.

For most, the path to citizenship begins with obtaining a permanent residence visa and with residing in the country for at least 5 years. (Those married to a Mexican citizen will be able to qualify for citizenship sooner).

Before you are approved for Mexican citizenship, you have to take a relatively simple exam about Mexican history and politics. In order to pass the exam (which is mandatory for citizenship), you need to have at least a basic understanding of Spanish.

Important! The US allows dual citizenship, so you don't have to surrender your US citizenship to become a Mexican citizen. Some European countries, however, do not allow dual citizenship, so consider this when applying if you are an EU citizen.

Once you file the initial application for citizenship, the procedure may take a year or longer to complete.

To find out more about becoming a Mexican Citizen, it's best to start with your local Mexican Consulate and go from there. The advice from the consulate is free, and only costs you the expense of your time and the trip. Since legal residency is required first, you will have plenty of time to consider whether you want to take this final step.

Expat Story: Applying for Permanent Residency

I moved to Playa Del Carmen in 2013, and decided to apply for permanent residency. I'd been back and forth to Playa dozens of times on vacation, and eventually decided to stay.

I believe that someone who lives here permanently really needs official residency status for banking, working, registering a vehicle, and so many other things. I hired an expert to help me. The immigration facilitator was recommended to me by someone I trust. I paid about $275 dollars for him to help me through the paperwork process. It was worth every penny, I swear. I also paid a translator to translate my documents, and that cost another $175. The entire process took several months to complete, but it wasn't difficult with the help of the facilitator. It was worth it, and made living and working in this area so much easier.

-Janet, Expat from the US.

Housing in Playa del Carmen

Before you decide to move to Playa del Carmen, remember that prices in the city have risen in the past several years. Due to an increased number of expats in the area, real estate in Playa is more in demand now than ever. That said, it's still possible to find reasonably priced real estate in Mexico, and beachfront property in Playa remains more affordable than in coastal cities in US.

If you are considering moving to Playa, you should definitely try to visit the city in person first. Most expats choose to rent a house in Playa for several months to a year before taking the plunge and making their move permanent. You want to be sure that you really love Playa before moving there, so plan an extended exploratory trip first.

Securing Affordable Housing

The most time-consuming part of moving to Playa is finding a place to rent or a property to buy. But don't worry. If you take your time, you can find an affordable home in Playa.

One strategy that works well when negotiating the price for an apartment is to start by asking the rent price and then haggle for a better price. Although it might seem crazy, most landlords will end up accepting the lower offer.

If you want to get the best price that you can on an apartment, make sure not to look during August, December, or January and to also avoid the times around Easter and Spring Break. During these times, higher demand causes rental prices to rise.

Housing in Playa del Carmen usually costs about 50% of what people pay for similar space and quality in the US. For instance, you can expect to find a lovely and well-equipped 1-bedroom apartment for just $500 per month. For a 2-bedroom apartment in downtown Playa or near the beach, expect to pay at least $900.

If you don't want to work with a real estate agency to rent an apartment in Playa, the following websites contain a great deal of information and listings that will simplify your search:

www.andale.mx

www.vivanuncios.com.mx

If you decide that you want to buy a property in Playa del Carmen, make sure you do your homework before signing any contracts. Working with a professional real estate agent is the best way to ensure that your purchase goes smoothly.

Many expats end up paying somewhere between $700 and $1000 per month depending on the size and exact location of the property.

Visiting Playa ahead of time gives you an opportunity to get to know the city's neighborhoods and determine which one is best suited to your preferences and budget. Exploring the city also helps you get a feel for the locals. Many who search for housing in Playa make the mistake of limiting their search to properties that are either within walking distance of the beach or that are along 5th Avenue, but there are many other great (and less expensive) options worth considering. Consider choosing a home that is a little further away from the beach in order to save on housing costs.

If you want to save money on rentals, don't limit your search to English-language websites, like Craigslist. These websites are focused on attracting tourists, who usually pay above-market prices. Expats on a budget should take the time to search Spanish-language sites that are oriented toward the locals.

It's also a good idea to walk the streets and look for signs advertising properties for sell and for rent. In fact, the best way to find an apartment or house in Playa is to search the city in person.

If you are trying to rent a house or apartment, contact local owners instead of those "vacation rental" companies. If you speak Spanish, you can negotiate with the owners directly. If you don't speak Spanish, try to find a friend or acquaintance that does, since local owners are often willing to give Spanish-speaking buyers what they call a "discount for locals."

If you are looking to buy property instead, your best bet is to work with a trusted real estate agent in Playa (see our exclusive interview with Laura Zapata of Seaview Properties, later).

Most real estate in Playa is sold by local realty agents, who know the area and all the steps that need to be taken for a successful real estate transaction. However, you can also buy a home directly from developers, especially if you're looking for beachfront property or a house located near a golf course.

Renting in Playa del Carmen

The most important thing to remember when renting a place in Playa is that you should always check it out in person before handing over any money. You should also be careful never to send a deposit before seeing a property in person.

More people rent properties in Playa than buy them, and many property owners prefer renting out their vacation properties part of the year. As a result, there are many rental properties available, and they can vary considerably when it comes to price and quality.

Renting a house based on images you have seen online is not the best idea, as you may find that the pictures the seller posted do not accurately represent the property. Visiting a property in person also helps you to get a good feel for the neighborhood.

Get Help Finding Rental Properties

Real Estate Agents: Local real estate agents keep an updated list of available properties and are often the easiest way to find a place to rent. That said, it's a good idea to check more than one agency's list; some places are listed for different prices with different agencies, while others are listed at some agencies but not at others. Real estate agents can also tell you about the different neighborhoods in Playa and can help you find the one that is best for your lifestyle and budget.

Newspapers and Internet Cafe Billboards: Newspapers and internet cafes are some most popular ways for locals to advertise their properties and for expats to find a place to rent. However, many expats (who are used to searching for things online at home) often overlook these sources of information.

Locals: Getting in touch with locals in restaurants and cafes is a great way to make connections and get information about possible rental properties. Locals often know things about neighborhoods and properties that can be hard to find out as a foreigner.

"Se Renta" Signs: Some homes will display for rent signs accompanied by a phone number. If you love the neighborhood and the look of the building, then go ahead and give the seller (or real estate agent) a call. If the sign belongs to a real estate agent, you will have to pay a commission. Handwritten signs are more likely to come from the seller directly.

Hotels: If you stay in a hotel while looking for a place to rent in Playa, then the staff there might be able to put you in touch with a few real estate agencies or even with a local who can help you with your rental.

Before looking for a place to rent in Playa del Carmen, take the time to answer the following questions:

- Do you want to rent an apartment or a house?
- Do you want to live in downtown Playa or outside of town?
- Does the rental need to be located close to stores, markets, and other local services?
- Would you prefer to rent a property located in a gated community?
- What is your rental budget?

- How much are you prepared to pay for monthly utilities?

Before Signing a Rental Contract

Asking the right questions before signing a rental contract will help you avoid any unpleasant surprises down the road. The following are all good things to ask the first time you meet with a landlord.

Property Questions:

- What utilities are available? Electricity, water, gas? Which are included in the rent?
- What are the terms of the lease, and what is the minimum rental term?
- Is there a water pump? Is it manual or automatic?
- Is the plumbing working properly?
- Is the phone connected?
- Are there any maintenance problems with the property?
- Who will take care of the landscaping? Is it the tenant's responsibility?
- Does the property have a security alarm?

The most expensive utility in Playa is electricity. The cost of electricity varies with the season and is highest in the summer, when the days are the hottest. The cost of electricity also varies by location, and is more expensive downtown than in less crowded areas.

Other utilities are cheaper. Water service is inexpensive in Playa, and most families only spend about $10 per month unless they have a swimming pool.

Natural gas tanks are available for purchase from gas trucks that traverse the city. Gas can be purchased in tanks of 20 liters ($20) or 30 liters ($45). Many buildings have a stationary tank installed on the roof that can hold about 100 liters of gas, and many properties have an exterior gas tank that powers their gas stove and water heater.

Tip! Always keep receipts for all rental and utility payments, especially those made with cash. It's also a good idea to keep an inventory of the property with the agent or landlord, so that you are not held accountable for something that you didn't damage or lose.

Interview with a Real Estate Pro

Buying property in Playa del Carmen takes time but can also be a great investment. The value of a property in Mexico depends mostly on location, local infrastructure, and local amenities.

Laura Zapata, a native Texan and graduate of the University of Texas realized her dream of living in tropical Mexico. After moving from the Dallas area to Playa del Carmen, Laura formed Seaview Properties. Laura served three years as President of the real estate board (AMPI) for the Riviera Maya. Laura is a US expat and real estate professional, who has a lot of great information for those thinking of buying property in Playa.

Interview with Laura Zapata of Seaview Properties

Expat Status: Expat in Playa del Carmen for over 20 Years

Q: Why don't you tell us a little bit about yourself, Laura?

Laura: I'm a real estate professional, and the name of my company is Seaview Properties. I've been doing business in the Riviera Maya for 20 years. We concentrate on Playa and the surrounding areas. We sell everything from empty lots to condos.

Q: You're originally from the United States right?

Laura: That's right; originally from Texas. But I've been living and working in Mexico for over 2 decades now.

Q: That's a long time. So when people look for a place to live in the Riviera Maya, do they generally prefer Playa del Carmen over neighboring cities like Tulum or Paamul?

Laura: Playa del Carmen is more populous than those other cities, and more people move there than to Tulum or Paamul. They've only begun to build in Tulum the last few years. Tulum recently became its own municipality, so there was a bit of a construction boom down there recently. Up and down the coast, there's been more construction activity in the last couple of years.

Q: Do you get a lot of questions about residency and moving?

Laura: It depends on the person. Not everyone plans on becoming a permanent resident. A lot of people buy property to come down for just a few months a year. We call them "snowbirds," because they come down for the winter and go back to the US whenever they want. Most of the people who plan to become residents will usually rent for a while; they're not homebuyers initially.

Q: You also manage several rentals. Are the owners of those properties people who purchased a vacation property for themselves and then contacted you to rent them out?

Laura: Yes, they are. For the most part, when people buy property here, they plan to move down in the future. They may come down for a few months every year, or they may come down for a couple of years. But some of them miss their grandkids, or something like that. So there are people who come down and stay for a while, and others purchase in order to retire later. There are all kinds of scenarios. By the time buyers are ready to retire, their property has often increased in value too.

Q: Do you feel it's easy for expats to purchase a home in Playa del Carmen? Or are there like a lot of road blocks?

Laura: It's not difficult to purchase real estate at all. It's a bit different from purchasing real estate in the US or Canada, but there aren't any road blocks or anything like that. Sometimes they have to set up a bank trust in order to purchase. The initial cost of set up is about $2,500 a year and then to maintain the trust, it's about $700 a year. It's not a lot of money compared to the property taxes you might pay in the US. If you look at how low the property taxes are here, it all evens out.

Q: Now, what's your opinion on the area itself? Do you feel like Playa del Carmen is safe?

Laura: Oh definitely. It's very safe. I've always been really comfortable here. In fact, I had more fear of my surroundings in the US than I do down here.

Q: What is your opinion of the surrounding areas like Playacar? Do you feel like those areas are as nice as Playa del Carmen?

Laura: Actually, Playacar is considered part of Playa del Carmen. It's just a private development within the city limits. They started developing it about 23 years ago, and it just grew from there. There are a lot of condos available in Playacar. It's a very nice area for expats. It's also well-maintained.

Q: What about family life? Do you feel like Playa del Carmen is a good place to bring kids?

Laura: Oh, it's lovely for children. Some people move down here and have their grandkids come down every summer. There are a lot of younger people moving to Playa del Carmen too; some don't have kids, but quite a few of them do. Those expats tend to not be buyers initially—young people in that age group. They're renters. There are good schools down here, which definitely encourages people to bring their families. Years ago, people had to go outside Playa del Carmen for private schools, but that's not the case anymore.

Q: Thanks for all the info. Before we go, do you have any general advice for people? Any final words of wisdom?

Laura: Most of the people who think about moving to Playa del Carmen have already been down here and loved it—they can't wait to come back. It's a little different down here, so you have to have a little patience. It's a different culture, and that's also what makes it nice. Leave yourself open to understanding other cultures and try and learn the language. Your adjustment will be easier if you make a little bit of effort ahead of time.

Buying a Home as a Foreigner

Foreigners can buy property in Mexico, but the private ownership of land by foreigners is restricted by law. Foreign nationals may only purchase land in the restricted border and coastal zones through a *fideicomiso* set up through a bank. A *fideicomiso* provides for the indirect ownership of land and property.

With a *fideicomiso*, when you buy property, the bank holds the title in a trust for 50 years. You and your heirs will be the sole beneficiaries of this trust (and the property), so you will be able to enjoy all the rights and privileges of ownership, including sale of the property, transfer of ownership, renting, leasing, and development. The *fideicomiso* can be renewed by you or your heirs for another 50 years. The trust also enables you to name a beneficiary upon your death, so you don't need to have a Mexican will for your heirs to inherit the property.

Where Should You Start?

The first step to buying a home in Mexico is to find a good realtor. Do your homework and choose a real estate agency that is reputable and trustworthy (we have included a list of realty companies in Playa del Carmen in the reference section of this book).

The process of purchasing property in Mexico is complicated and involves a great deal of paperwork. The legal aspects of the process can also be difficult to navigate, especially if you are not fluent in Spanish.

Regardless of the agency you choose, you should look for a local agent who knows the area well and with whom you can build a relationship based on trust.

What Kind of Property Do You Want to Buy?

Playa del Carmen offers a wide selection of properties. You can purchase land and build your own home, or you can choose to purchase a finished home. Most expats opt for a condo in a gated community or a new house situated a somewhere off the beach (which is more

77

affordable than one right on the water). Even with their maintenance fees, condos tend to be more affordable than homes in the same location; however, they offer less privacy and their resale value is not as good as a single-family home.

Pre-Sale Real Estate

Some expats prefer to invest in pre-sale real estate, which is property that is not yet finished or available. With so many new real estate developments in Playa, this practice is becoming increasingly popular.

Here are some of the reasons that expats choose pre-sale real estate:

- They get first choice on the location of the property when the presale starts.

- They benefit from incentives for buying upfront.

- They can customize the property before it's finished.

- They can choose finishes in advance without paying additional fees.

While there are good reasons for choosing pre-sale real estate, you still need to be cautious. Before buying a pre-sale property, make sure to do the following:

- Check the reputation of the developer. Make sure to buy from someone known for quality construction, respecting delivery terms, and offering proper legal paperwork.

- Check the area where the development is being built and research it thoroughly.

- Don't sell or rent your home back in the US until the property is actually finished; it's not at all unheard of for a developer to push back a delivery date.

Where Do You Want to Buy?

Most of the newer developments in Playa del Carmen are located approximately 10 minutes from the beach by car, so even if you can't afford a beachfront property, you will still be very close to a beach.

In Playa, Highway 307 is the line that divides cheaper properties from the more expensive ones. Most expats prefer to live in a property situated between the beach and the highway.

If you buy a place in downtown Playa, you will be able to get almost everywhere you need without a car or public transportation. Most of the residents who live downtown choose to walk or ride a bike.

Generally speaking, younger people in Playa prefer to buy real estate downtown, because they enjoy being close to the heart of the city. Meanwhile, older residents often prefer quieter neighborhoods that are situated farther away from the tourists.

Popular Communities in Playa

There are numerous popular areas to buy property in Playa del Carmen. Each is a good option for different reasons and has its own specific personality.

Playacar

Playacar is the trendiest district of Playa and has a modern atmosphere. There are condos, luxury homes, and upscale shops. It is an older development, and basic services are already well-established. You don't need a car to go grocery shopping, for example.

Playacar has nice beaches that are not too crowded and wide streets, which are great for biking and running. The district also has a private security force.

House prices in Playacar start around $300,000 and reach into the millions. If you're looking to buy a condo in this area, expect to pay at least $130,000 or more.

Colosio

Colosio is also one of the newer neighborhoods in downtown Playa.

This neighborhood is largely dedicated to condo developments. Many of the developments are not yet finished, so many expats purchase pre-sale properties in this area.

Colosio's main street has new lighting, a wide sidewalk, beautiful trees, and convenient benches. This neighborhood has plenty of parking. Colosio is also great for biking.

While Colosio is close to the beach, there are no beachfront properties in the neighborhood. The lot sizes in Colosio are not very large either, but this also keeps their costs down. Homes are more affordable overall in Colosio than they are in Playa.

Mareazul

Mareazul includes an ambitious development project to build a huge swath of waterfront condominiums to the area. Most of the condos in this area have ocean views or are within walking distance of the beach.

This neighborhood is situated at the north end of Playa del Carmen in a resort community. Mareazul offers condos for sale and for rent, so you can choose to live in this area for a short period and get a feel for the neighborhood. There are many 2-bedroom and 4-bedroom condos available in Mareazul, and some of its complexes have a spa, a gym, a garden, and outdoor entertainment.

Mareazul is situated about 10 minutes away from downtown Playa by car and has no stores or attractions within walking distance. This is resort area, and there are few amenities that do not cater directly to tourists. It is set in a tranquil area, but living here would require a car to travel into the city.

La Quinta (Downtown)

Also known as 5th Avenue, La Quinta is the center of local tourism. This street runs parallel to the beach. This area is home to many restaurants, bars, and souvenir shops. Prices are higher in this area than anywhere else in Playa del Carmen, but expats like to visit and live here to enjoy the bustling activity and indulge in a nice meal or the local nightlife.

Living downtown is expensive, and a simple 2-bedroom condo will average around $250,000 and go up from there to several million dollars.

Why Do You Want to Buy?

Before figuring out which community is right for you, there are several things you have to consider. How long you are planning to live in Playa as well as whether or not you are planning to rent out your property are both factors that will affect your purchasing decision.

If you're planning to live in Playa for at least a few years, purchase a property in an area where real estate values are on the rise. Even if you want to stay in your new home in Playa forever, it's a good idea to consider properties that will prove to be a good investment down the road.

As mentioned earlier, most real estate transactions in Playa are settled in cash, and it's uncommon for people to request a loan from a Mexican bank in order to finance the purchase of a home.

Mexican banks do offer mortgages for foreigners, but they also require substantial down payments and often come with interest rates that are considerably higher than those in the US.

Other Things to Consider Before Buying a Home

Termites

Thanks to the humid weather in Mexico, termites are a rather common problem in the Mexican Riviera. Many wooden structures are vulnerable to these pests, but the best contractors use tropical hardwoods that are termite-resistant. Brick homes are also common in Playa, as they termite resistant.

Tropical Hurricanes

Buildings in Playa are built to withstand tropical hurricanes. That said, hurricanes do happen, and damage from them is possible. If you are worried about hurricanes, make sure that your home has quality hurricane shutters and a sturdy roof. You may also want to consider purchasing property a little farther form the water.

Climate

Since the weather is usually hot in Playa, it is a good idea to purchase property with good ventilation, high ceilings, ceiling fans, and air conditioning. You should also consider picking property with mature shade trees and shaded exterior windows.

Moisture

Playa has relatively high levels of humidity, which means that mold is a common problem. Look for property with plenty of natural light and good airflow (especially in areas like closets). If you visit a property and see signs of mold or notice a musty smell, you probably shouldn't purchase it.

Avoiding Crime: Tips for Staying Safe in the Riviera Maya

The Riviera Maya—along with the entire Yucatan Peninsula—is one of the safest areas in Mexico.

According to a recently published report[1], almost all violent crime in Mexico occurs along the Mexico-US border and in the Northern Pacific Coast regions (such as Sinaloa, Michoacán, and Guerrero), where drug cartels are most active. The US state department warns travelers against visiting 4 out of Mexico's 31 states. These are: Chihuahua, Coahuila, Durango, and Tamaulipas. There are no such warnings for the Riviera Maya or the state of Quintana Roo, which are considered safe regions for Americans to visit. Take some time to research tips for traveling safely abroad before your departure.

Most tourist areas—including to Baja Sur, Cancun, Playa del Carmen, Tulum, Cabo San Lucas, Isla Mujeres, Cozumel, and Los Barriles—are safe, and have a good police presence that are dedicated to protecting the safety of tourists—and the revenue that they bring into these regions.

Crime in Mexico

Kidnappings in Mexico are rare, but they do happen. Physical kidnappings occur when a victim is physically abducted and is held for ransom. "Express" and "virtual" kidnappings also occur. Express kidnapping involves abducting victims for a short time and forcing them to withdraw money from an ATM. Virtual kidnapping is an extortion-by-deception crime, wherein a victim is contacted by phone and scammed into paying a ransom.

Carjacking and highway robbery are also serious problems in Mexico, but these crimes occur primarily along the border. Most incidents occur at night and on isolated roads, which is why the US State Department

---

[1] Stanford University's 2010 Report on violent crime in Mexico.

strongly urges travelers to travel between cities only during daylight hours, to avoid isolated roads, and to use toll roads (*cuotas*) whenever possible.

Playa is not a dangerous city, but it always pays to be cautious. Even though Playa is safe, crimes do happen there (as they do everywhere).

Misinformed opinions and rumors can't replace actual facts, and you should always do your own research before making judgments about a place that you are not familiar with.

Here are some reliable government sources for updated travel information:

- travel.state.gov

- travel.gc.ca

- www.gov.uk

If you still aren't sure if you will feel safe in Playa, talk to some expats in the area. You can easily connect with people who live in Playa online, as there are many forums and blogs dedicated to moving, living, and retiring there.

Crime in Playa is usually nonviolent and does not result in fatalities. While the likelihood of any individual expat being a victim of a crime is not particularly high, there are things you can do to increase your safety. Most of the crimes that happen in this area are property crimes like theft and burglary, so it pays to safeguard your belongings. Burglary is mostly a crime of opportunity, which means that it is also one of the easiest to prevent.

Get to Know Your Neighbors

Getting to know your neighbors is great for making friends and learning the language, but it can also be a good way to increase your security. If your neighbors know you (and especially if they like you), they are more likely to intervene if they see anything suspicious happening in or around your property. Knowing your neighbors also helps if you ever need to leave your home unoccupied for an extended period of time, since you can ask them check on your property and collect your mail while you're gone.

Metal Window Protectors

Many people in Playa leave their windows (and even their doors) open to let in the breeze, but if your windows aren't protected, burglars might easily enter through them—especially if you live on the ground floor. If you own a home or a condo where window protectors are allowed, don't hesitate to install them; in addition to deterring thieves, they also provide additional protection during hurricanes.

An unlocked door is basically an invitation for burglars, so exercising a little common sense by keeping your door locked can go a long way. It's also a good idea to keep your keys away from open windows or doors, so that they cannot be obtained from the outside.

Don't Be a Show-Off

It's always wise to keep your valuable possessions inside and in a place where they can't be seen by people passing by. Keep curtains and blinds closed (especially at night or when no one is home), and store things you can't replace or that have a particularly high value in a secure location. It's also a good idea to keep valuable possession out of the site of any contractors. You should also spend the extra money required to hire reputable companies whenever you need work done in your home.

Tip! Always store tools and ladders in a secure location, like a locked shed or garage. Don't make it easier for someone to rob you by giving them access to the tools to do it.

Don't Be Too Predictable

Most people live according to a routine, but it's a good idea to vary your patterns just a bit, since doing so can prevent potential thieves from growing confident about when your home will be empty. If you have to follow a set schedule, try occasionally leaving your lights or TV on while you are away to deter thieves.

Exterior Lights and Motion Detectors

No matter where you live, exterior lights and motion detectors can help increase your peace of mind. Exterior motion detectors are cheap, and can be installed without a professional electrician. If you do install a motion detector light, get one that allows you to adjust the sensitivity so that it doesn't annoy your neighbors by turning on too often.

Tip! You might consider installing an alarm system too, but if you choose to forgo an alarm but still want to know if anyone approaches your house, adopting a guard dog might be a better solution.

How to Avoid Getting Ripped Off

Since expats and tourists are less likely to know the real prices of things than locals, they can fall victim to overcharging without even realizing it. When you first arrive in Playa, don't buy the first things you see. Instead, take the time to visit several stores, so you can get a better idea of what the items you need usually cost. If you know what something is really worth in Playa, then stores won't be able to take advantage of you. Exploring is also a good way to find deals. Furthermore, while prices are usually fixed in Playa, you can negotiate with some of the street vendors.

When Dining Out

Mexican law does not allow restaurants to add supplementary charges to the prices advertised on their menus, but they sometimes try to anyway. This is especially true in tourist areas (like Playa's 5th Avenue), so look your bill over carefully before paying. You should also look your bill over carefully to see whether or not it includes the tip (which is allowed) and should check the price of dishes and drinks before you order them. If you notice any special offers, find out exactly what they include before ordering (if an offer sounds too good to be true, then it probably is).

When Taking a Taxi

Taxi drivers all over the world are known for overcharging foreigners. Taxis in Playa don't have meters; their rates are based on a chart, which you should use to find out the rates for the area you want to travel to. If you just ask drivers for the price, some of them might add about 5 pesos or more to the total rate. They could also overcharge you at night, especially if they notice that you are intoxicated.

What to Do if You're the Victim of a Crime

The emergency (police, ambulance, and fire) phone number for the Riviera Maya is 066. Although there may be English-speaking operators available, finding a Spanish speaker to assist you or to make the call for you can save a lot of time.

When US citizens are the victims of a serious crime in Mexico, the US State Department recommends that they contact the local police or the nearest US embassy, consulate, or consular agency.

What the US Embassy in Mexico Can Do for You

- It can replace a stolen passport. The loss or theft of a US passport abroad should be immediately reported to the local police and to the nearest US Embassy or Consulate.

- It can help you find appropriate medical care if you are the victim of violent crimes like assault and rape.

- It can put you in contact with the appropriate police authorities and contact family members or friends on your behalf.

- It can help you understand the local criminal justice process and direct you to local attorneys. Under the best of circumstances, prosecution is very difficult (a fact some assailants seem to exploit), and no criminal investigation is possible without a formal complaint to Mexican authorities.

If you want to stay safe abroad, then you should also consider doing the following:

- Enroll in the Smart Traveler Enrollment Program, so you can stay up-to-date on all important safety and security announcements.

- Follow the Bureau of Consular Affairs on Twitter and Facebook.

- Bookmark the Bureau of Consular Affairs website, which contains the current Travel Warnings and Travel Alerts as well as the Worldwide Caution.

- In the event of an emergency, you can contact the US State Department at 1 888 407 4747 (toll-free within the US and Canada) or at 1 202 501 4444.

Got Kids? A Guide to Local Schools

If you are relocating to Playa with children, then you will need to do some research before determining which school is right for them. Not only will you need to find a quality school that offers English instruction, but you will also need to find one that fits the specific needs and personalities of your children. Ideally, you should already know which school your kids will be attending before you relocate permanently.

What Education is Best for Your Children?

If you're planning to stay for an undetermined period, then you should consider enrolling them in a private school. Private school curriculum immerses children in Mexican culture and helps them quickly adjust to their new home. Most private schools teach their curriculum in both English and Spanish.

If you want to spend only a few months in Playa del Carmen, then you should try to arrange an online program with your children's existing US school, so that they can keep up with the work they will miss. If their school is unwilling to offer such a program, then there are also plenty of "homeschool" online learning programs that you can enroll your children in that will keep their education on track.

If you're planning to stay for more than 6 months but aren't planning to make Playa your permanent home, you can also look for private schools that offer intermediate programs for students who will be attending their courses on a temporary basis.

No matter what sort of education you choose for your children, you should find a local tutor to help them learn Spanish quickly. Allowing them to take part in extracurricular sports or arts programs is also a good way to help them make local friends and improve their language skills.

The younger your children are, the easier it will be for them to adjust to a new culture and environment. Kids make friends quickly and learn a new language much faster than older children and adults.

However, if your children are already in middle school or high school, then they may find the experience of making friends and fitting in to a new school frustrating, especially if they don't speak fluent Spanish.

It is not uncommon for expats to homeschool or enroll their children in online programs, especially if they want them to attend a university in the US and need them to focus on getting a good SAT score or maintaining a high GPA.

Younger kids stand to benefit greatly from attending a school where they will be surrounded by Mexican culture and by other children, but for older teens may prefer to continue a course of education similar to the one in their home country.

Childhood Education in Mexico

The Mexican government is dedicated to maintaining high standards in all of its educational institutions. Mexico prides itself on its high literacy rate and is also determined to help students excel in math and the sciences.

Public schools in Mexico are funded by the government, while the private schools rely mostly on private funding.

All children who live in Mexico are allowed to attend Mexican public schools, but only Mexican citizens may attend free of charge. If you want to enroll your children in a Mexican public school, you will need to comply with numerous requirements and will also need to pay tuition.

Tip! Middle and upper class Mexican families prefer to enroll their children in private schools in order expose them to a customized curriculum in a bilingual (or even trilingual) education system. Private schools also offer more extracurricular activities and sports.

Grade Levels in Mexico

Grade levels in Mexico don't differ much from those in the United States. However, Mexicans are allowed to place their children in a preschool classroom once they reach the age of 2, which means that they often start attending school earlier than the American kids. Additionally, preschool education is mandatory for children ages 3 through 6 in Mexico.

Preschool through secondary school are compulsory and free for Mexican citizens. School uniforms are also obligatory. However, unlike in the United States, high school is not mandatory in Mexico. Most high schools (called *preparatorias)* are found in urban areas. Students who attend high school can choose either to get a vocational certificate or a diploma.

Where grades in the US are given as letters from A to F, Mexico uses a number system (10 to 5).

Note! Parents aren't as involved in school decisions in Mexico as they are in the United States. There are no parent-teacher conferences in Mexico, and parents are only invited to school whenever there is the need for volunteers and contributions. They are not allowed to be members of school boards, and school decisions are made without them.

School Calendar in Mexico

The Mexican school year begins in mid-August and ends in late June or early July.

Summer break is only 45 days long. In addition to the short breaks between terms, there are also several 2-day breaks for various religious celebrations and governmental holidays. The Easter vacation (called the *Semana Santa*) is sometimes 2 full weeks, and Christmas vacation usually lasts for 3 weeks.

6 Steps to Choosing the Right School for your Kids

1. Do Your Research Early

The internet and established expats are some of the best sources of information about schools in Playa del Carmen. Visit online forums, where you can ask families who have lived in Playa about their experiences there. Your realtor or immigration lawyer should also be able to recommend schools to you.

2. Prepare the Required Documents

You should know what documents you need to enroll your children in schools in Playa del Carmen and have them ready before your departure. These documents usually include a birth certificate, vaccination record, certificate of good health from a pediatrician, and school records. Most schools require these documents to be "apostilled," so make sure you take care of this before heading to Playa del Carmen.

> **Note!** An apostille is a document authenticated by a public official (Usually the Secretary of State). In this way, it is similar to a notary stamp. The cost of having a document apostilled varies from state to state. In California, it costs about $25 to have a document (such as a birth certificate) apostilled and processing by mail usually takes 2-3 weeks.

3. Contact the schools

Once you have a list of preferred schools, get in touch with them as soon as possible. Email each of the schools you are interested in and ask them any questions you might have.

4. Visit Schools and Speak to Administrators

Make at least 1 trip to Playa to visit schools before moving there. Set up interviews with the school administrators and ask if you can observe a class to get a sense of the educational atmosphere. Write down your impressions of each school, so that you can compare them all later.

5. Narrow Down the List

Once you have chosen a few schools that might be great for your children, you should set up interviews for them and also arrange for your children to sit in on a few classes. Regardless of your children's Spanish-speaking abilities, they will usually be placed in classrooms according to their age, rather than their academic level.

Note: We've compiled a detailed list of Playa schools in the reference section in the back of this book, designed to make your search for the best school easier.

Banking in Mexico

Mexico is primarily a cash-based economy, and most transactions there, including real estate transactions, continue to be made in cash to this day. Credit and debit cards are gaining popularity in Mexico, but they are more commonly used by expats than by Mexican nationals.

Mexico's official currency is the peso. Pesos are printed in denominations of 20, 50, 100, 200, 500 and 1,000. At the time of this book's printing, the US dollar was valued at about 13 pesos. Many tourist areas will also accept American dollars or Euros, but expect a lower exchange rate if you pay with non-Mexican currency.

Banks in Mexico are notorious for high interest rates, bank fees, and poor level of customer service. These are just some of the many reasons that many expats prefer to maintain their foreign bank accounts while using local ATMs to withdraw cash.

Mexicans banks provide most of the same services as US banks, but their fees and commissions work differently. Internet banking is starting to become more popular in Mexico, but online banking is not as ubiquitous as it is stateside. Most Mexicans still pay their bills (power, water, telephone, internet, etc.) in cash and in person.

However, having a Mexican bank account is helpful if you want to get a job in Mexico, or transfer money for large purchases, such as a car or a home.

There are many banks in Mexico, and most of them are foreign-owned. Some of the larger and more popular banks are the Canadian-owned *Scotiabank*, the European *Santander*, and the Mexican *Banorte*.

Some banks cater to expats. For example, *Lloyd Bank* (which has branches in the Chapala area and in San Miguel de Allende) provides specialized services to foreigners and offers deposit services for US checks.

There are multiple banks in Playa del Carmen and the surrounding areas. Do a little footwork and visit a several banks in person to find the one that's right for you.

Opening a Mexican Bank account

To open a bank account in Mexico, you need proof of Mexican residency (a temporary or permanent residence visa), proof of address, and a passport. Most banks ask clients to pay a monthly fee or to maintain a minimum balance. Expats usually choose to open a simple deposit account that allows them to deposit and withdraw money from ATMs. Each bank allows a certain number of free ATM withdrawals before charging a fee for transactions.

You can also open a checking account that includes a checkbook, but such accounts come with higher fees or with higher balance minimums than basic deposit (savings) accounts.

> **Important:** You can't open a Mexican bank account with a visitor's visa. However, you can use an ATM card issued by an American bank to withdraw money from most Mexican ATMs. Expect to pay a fee.

Credit Cards and Debit Cards

Use of credit cards in Mexico is still somewhat unusual. Although most businesses accept credit cards in tourist areas, most small shops and businesses in outlying towns only accept cash.

This is partly because Mexican banks usually charge a high percentage on sales paid with a credit card (around 7%), which makes accepting credit cards impractical for many small businesses. In Mexico, you will find many restaurants, bars, and shops that only accept cash. Places that do accept credit cards include hotels, high-end restaurants, gas stations, and most shops in tourist zones.

Access to ATM Machines

Most ATMs charge fees for withdrawals made with cards issued by foreign banks, but this is not always the case. For example, Bank of

America has an arrangement with Scotiabank and Santander in Mexico, which allows Bank of America customers to use their cards at those banks' ATMs without paying a fee.

> **Important!** If an ATM machine retains your card for any reason, the card will be destroyed by the bank, and you will have to get a new one. So make sure you have a back-up card (like a credit card) that you can use in case of emergency.

Money Transfers

Wire transfers are the safest method for moving large amounts of money. Most banks charge a flat wire fee. To make such a transfer, you will need the ABA or SWIFT code for the receiving institution, the account holder's name, and the account number.

Simple money transfers using a third-party service (like Western Union, Money Gram, and Xoom) are better for small amounts of money (amounts under $3,000 dollars). These companies provide money wire services in minutes. You can send money online, via telephone, or in person at an office. Fees are based on the amount you send.

Moving Your Stuff

Are you ready to move? Do you want to take your stuff with you? The Mexican government will allow you a one-time wavier of the import duties on your household items.

You will be required to draft a detailed list of your household belongings when you import them into Mexico. This is called the "Menaje de Casa" and it allows you to transfer your used household belongings. You must sort, pack, and inventory all you belongings in boxes. All the boxes must be clearly labeled for the Menaje.

If you're planning to move to Playa for good, this waiver is all you need.

New items will be subject to import taxes, so if you have a lot of items still in their original boxes, then expect to pay a fee for those.

Many expats have a hard time deciding what to bring with them to Playa and aren't sure how to move most of their belongings.

> **Tip!** Visit aduanas.gob.mx for more details about customs allowances and for tips for transporting your belongings into Mexico.

The *Menaje de Casa* paperwork should be provided by the Mexican Consulate.

Preparing Your List

If you decide to take most of your belongings with you, prepare for a lot of packing, labelling, and numbering. All small belongings should go into boxes, which must be numbered, labeled, and inventoried for the *Menaje*.

> **Important!** The *Menaje de Casa* has to be written in Spanish, so make sure you label your boxes in both English and Spanish and write the list in Spanish. If you don't know Spanish, ask someone who does to assist you.

The original list and several copies must be submitted to the Mexican Consulate for approval and stamping. The application fee is around $130. To learn more about this procedure, contact your nearest Mexican Consulate directly.

Prohibited Items

You can't bring the following items into Mexico:

- Firearms and ammunition, except for hunting purposes and only if you respect the rules specified in Section 4 of the Manual of Tourist Entry. You must first apply for a permit at a Mexican Consulate to bring a rifle for hunting (or any other firearm) into the country.
- Fresh or frozen meat
- Cheese, eggs, milk, or other dairy products
- Plants and plant material (including fruits, vegetables, seeds, and spices)

You can't export or import the following items from or into Mexico:

- Live predatory fish of any age (like piranhas)
- Turtle skins, loggerhead turtles, or turtle eggs
- Poppy seeds or juice or extracts of opium.
- Marijuana, including seeds, extracts, oils, or medication prepared with marijuana
- Thallium sulfate (a rodenticide used against mice and rats)
- Insecticide
- Medication prepared with acetylmorphine or any of its salts or derivatives

Who is Going to Move Your Belongings?

The easiest way to get all of your stuff to Mexico is to hire a moving company and let them deal with the packing and transportation of your belongings. However, if you are travelling by car, then you may want to move your things yourself using a vehicle or trailer.

Moving to Mexico—a DIY Job?

Important! You can't take a rental truck (like a U-Haul) into Mexico, so you'll need to use your own vehicle if you want to move your belongings yourself. If you use a trailer, it needs to be listed on your vehicle permit, and you will also have to have proof of ownership of the trailer.

Moving your household items across the border is not a simple process. Expat experiences vary, but some have found it to be quite stressful. This is something that you should consider carefully before deciding how to move your belongings. Here are some moving tips:

- Learn to let go! Don't be a packrat! Take only what you really need. The more you bring with you, the more complicated and the more expensive the moving process will be.

- There is a limit on the amount of luggage that can be taken per person.

- In addition to packing and transporting, you will also need to take care of loading and unloading (which may require you to navigate stairs, narrow hallways, and bad roads with your belongings).

Using a Moving Company

Before picking a mover, get quotes from several companies that have good reputations and that provide the services you need.

You can find plenty of moving companies that specialize in moving expats overseas.

Important! Measure all big items so that you know exactly how big they are and can determine whether they will fit in your boxes. A removal company can ask you to pay more than previously agreed if your stuff takes up more space than discussed.

> **Tip!** If you are moving only a few items and if the total value of dutiable items is less than $3,000, then you can skip the *Menaje*, because it won't be worth the effort.

Tips for Crossing the Border:

- Don't bring large quantities of any single item, because this will suggest that you intend to resell them, and they will be confiscated.

- Don't try to smuggle any narcotics or illicit drugs into Mexico. You will get caught and will end up in jail.

- If you're planning to bring a gun into Mexico, make sure you have a special permit issued by the Mexican Consulate, because US firearms licenses are not valid in Mexico.

Moving Your Pets

Mexican customs will allow you to bring your pets into Mexico as long as you respect several rules and have the right paperwork.

> **Important!** Only 2 pets are allowed per person.

The most common pets that people bring with them to Playa are dogs and cats. To bring them into Mexico, an owner must have the following documents:

- **International Certificate of Good Health (Form 77-043):** This document must be issued by a licensed veterinarian, and the vet must provide a letter on letterhead containing his professional license number and signature. The certificate needs to be issued no more than 5 days before the animal enters Mexico

- **Proof of Vaccinations:** You must prove that your pet has been vaccinated against rabies, distemper, hepatitis, and leptospirosis, and all vaccinations need to have been administrated at least 15 days (but no more than 1 year) before the pet enters Mexico. Dates of vaccination must be provided along with the owner's name and address and a complete description of the pet.

Once you get to Mexico, your pet will be screened at an Animal and Plant Health Inspection Office; these offices are situated at international airports, border crossings, and international seaports. The office will determine if the animal should be allowed immediate entry or should remain in custody for additional inspection.

If the animal can enter Mexico immediately, it will be issued an animal importation certificate (Certificado Zoosanitario), which you should keep, as you will need it if you ever leave Mexico with the animal. If the animal needs to remain in custody, the office will give you a voucher. As long as you have the right paperwork, the chances of your animal being detained are quite slim.

Transporting Pets by Plane

When traveling by air, pets need to be transported in sturdy crates (cats) or kennels (dogs). Airlines will not allow you to transport a pet in cardboard, plastic boxes, or other non-secure containers. Some airline companies allow certain pets to travel in the cabin with their owner for an additional fee, so check with your airline ahead of time. Crates and kennels need to be properly labeled with the following:

- Your full name

- Your permanent address

- Your telephone number

The crate should indicate which way is up and should also have the word "LIVE ANIMALS" prominently displayed on it. Your pet should also wear its tags when in transit.

The pet's transport container should be clean and should not contain any bedding, cloth, or other materials. You are not allowed to place food or water inside the crate or kennel either, but you can include dishes where the airline staff can place food and water. You may bring a day's ration of dried food or an unopened bag of food. Food must be properly sealed and labeled in English or Spanish

Airline fees for bringing a pet into Mexico vary from company to company. If you have a large dog and if the combined weight of the kennel and animal is greater than 100 lbs., then the pet may have to be transported as cargo.

Animals Other than Dogs and Cats

You can bring other animals into Mexico, including birds, but only if you respect all the requirements imposed by the SAGARPA-SENASICA. There are stricter requirements for animals that aren't cats or dogs. Additionally, the animal may be subject to a 40-day quarantine, tests, and vaccines, and you will probably have to obtain additional health certificates.

Reference Section

Publisher's Note: No website or company has paid a fee in order to be mentioned in reference section. All the information in this section is intended for educational purposes only and cannot be considered legal advice. Expats and those considering expatriation should consult professional legal and tax advisors if they have any questions.

Realty Companies

The following informational chart lists popular realty companies in Playa del Carmen.

Real Estate Agency	Services	Contact Information
Seaview Properties	This family-owned business provides buyer broker services for Playa del Carmen, the Riviera Maya, and properties on the Costa Maya. It also offers long-term rentals and vacation rentals	US: 361 877 7279 MX Office: 984 879 3107 MX Cell: 984 876 2134 seaviewprop.com
Caribbean Realty	This agency specializes in real estate and vacation rentals in Playa del Carmen and the Riviera Maya area.	+52 984 873 5218 Info@PuertoAventurasRentals.com puertoaventurasrentals.com
Mexico Realty Investment	This agency specializes in working with foreign investors and developers in both commercial and residential Mexican real estate. The agents speak English, Spanish, French, Italian, and Polish	From the US: +1 646.355.3698; +1 512.539.0209 From Canada: +1 604.771.8306 mexicorealtyinvestment.com
Playa Citizen	This real estate agency focuses on properties specifically in Playa del Carmen.	Office: +52 984-803-3300 Cell: +52 984-116-9696 US: +1 281-770-5258 playacitizenrealestate.com
Playa Rentals	**This agency offers long-term rentals and vacation rental services. The owner speaks English, Spanish, and German.**	**Office: +52 984-803-0636** **Cell: +52 984-135-4129** **info@playa-rentals.com** **playa-rentals.com**
Croc Condos	This agency specializes in affordable 1-bedroom and studio rentals.	+52 984-745-0274 croccondos@gmail.com croccondos.shutterfly.com

Latido de Mexico	This agency offers long-term rentals and property management services.	+52 984-876-3215 info@latidodemexico.com latidodemexico.com
Resorts Real Estate	This experienced agency focuses on pre-construction ownership opportunities, resort real estate, and re-sales in the Riviera Maya.	Mexico: +52 984-116-3251 From US: +1 800-441-3275 From Canada and Worldwide: +1 604-628-7247 udi@resorts-real-estate.com playadelcarmenrealestatemexico.com
Top Mexico Real Estate	This agency specializes in providing real estate services to English-speaking buyers.	+52 984-267-2449 US: +1 512-879-6546 info@topmexicorealestate.com topmexicorealestate.com

Private Health Insurance Companies in Mexico

Mexico has a variety of insurance companies that provide private health coverage for a monthly fee. Each insurance company has different health care plans, which offer a variety of coverage levels depending on your needs. Policies are also adjusted for age.

Insurance company	Contact Information
Allianz Mexico	allianz.com.mx
Royal & Sun Mexico	royalsun.com.mx
MetLife Mexico	metlife.com.mx
DKV	dkvseguros.com
Grupo Inbursa	inbursa.com
International Medical Group	imglobal.com
AXA Seguro	MX: 01 800 001 8700 , US and Canada: 1 888 293 7221
HCC Medical Insurance Services	worldtrips.com

Private Schools that Teach English and Spanish

This is not an exhaustive list and is informational only. The authors of this book do not endorse any particular school in Playa del Carmen.

Ak Lu'Um International School

Phone: 984 115 4367
Email: info@akluum.com
Website: *akluum.com*
Education Levels: kindergarten, preschool, and primary school

Ak Lu'Um International School is affiliated with the AWSNA (Association of Waldorf Schools of North America) and Latin American Waldorf Schools. It is the only non-profit school in the area and accepts students on scholarships.

The school offers a bilingual program in English and Spanish and a curriculum based exclusively on the Waldorf pedagogy and the teachings of humanist Rudolf Steiner. The school also has an eco-friendly jungle campus situated just south of Playa del Carmen, near Xcaret.

All teachers are bilingual, and children learn both English and Spanish. A third language (French or German) may be introduced in Grade 1. Children are also exposed to a variety of indoor and outdoor games and are encouraged to take part in numerous activities.

Centro Comunitario Otoch Paal Montessori

Phone: 984 130 0920
Email: otochpaalmontessori@yahoo.com
Website: *montessoridecancun.com/akumal*
Education Levels: preschool only

This private preschool opened in 2004 and has 3 classrooms. One of the kindergarten classrooms follows a bilingual curriculum and teaches both English and Spanish.

Colegio Ingles

Phone: 984 267 2897
Email: English Coordinator, english@colegioingles-qroo.com.mx
Website: *colegioingles-qroo.com.mx*
Education Levels: preschool, primary, secondary, and high school

Colegio Ingles is an accredited private school that offers bilingual education in English and Spanish. The school has a large foreign student population and a campus equipped with a large pool, a soccer field, and an outdoor auditorium. It also offers students access to a variety of extracurricular activities like painting, jazz, ballet, theater, music, French, Taekwondo, and an impressive selection of other sports.

Colegio Montessori

Phone: 984 118 5866
Email: mplaya@infinitum.com.mx
Website: *selvamar.com.mx/colegio-montesori.html*
Education Levels: preschool, primary, and secondary school

This accredited school bases its curriculum on the Montessori principles and offers a bilingual program for its mix of national and foreign students. The school is located just north of Playa del Carmen on the premises of the Selvamar residential complex.

Colegio Puerto Aventuras

Phone: 984 873 5141
Email: gabi@pa.com.mx
Website: *colegiopuertoaventuras.com*
Education Levels: preschool, primary, secondary, and high school

Colegio Puerto Aventuras is an SEP bilingual educational institution situated within the gates of the Puerto Aventuras community. Although Puerto Aventuras houses many foreign families and although this school is perfect for Puerto Aventuras residents, it requires a bit of a commute for those in Playa.

The school has strong academic reputation, offers a multicultural environment, and is a favorite among Mexicans and expats alike. The school also offers the possibility for students to learn French and is equipped with a library, a language center, an IT center and laboratory, sports fields, and a cafeteria.

Comunidad Educativo El Papalote

Phone: 984 879 3052
Email: elpapalote@prodigy.net.mx
Website: *colegioelpapalote.edu.mx*
Education Levels: preschool, primary, secondary, and high school

El Papalote has been in operation for over 20 years and offers a great bilingual program as well as a variety of after-school activities, including dance, painting, and sports. The curriculum is based on the Waldorf program, and the school's philosophy reflects the cosmopolitan and multicultural atmosphere of Playa del Carmen. The school is located in the city center, and is one of most popular institutions for families new to the area.

Colegio Weston

Phone: 984 109 2216
Email: colegiowestonmx@hotmail.com
Website*: colegioweston.com*
Education Levels: maternal, preschool, primary, and secondary school

This SEP-accredited educational institution is a traditional Mexican private school that offers a trilingual scholar program. Its student body includes Americans and other foreigners as well as many Mexican nationals. The school also offers a variety of extracurricular activities including swimming, ballet, jazz, yoga, art, music, computer science, and Taekwondo. The school follows the Common Core Standard of the SEP program, as well as other programs meant to enrich the learning process. The school is equipped with soccer fields, volleyball and tennis courts, a pool, a science and IT laboratory, a library, and green areas.

Village Green Preschool

Phone: 984 206 2206 and 206-2226
Website: *greenvillageschool.com.mx*
Education Levels: kindergarten and preschool

Village Green Preschool provides bilingual courses for children 2-5 years old. This private school has air-conditioned rooms, security cameras, double door security, a farm, a garden, a pool, and IT rooms. The school also provides dining and first aid services and offers children opportunities to practice yoga, Taekwondo, and other sports.

Instituto Tepeyac Xcaret

Phone: 984 877 25 00
Email: cap.xcaret@tepeyac.mx
Website: *institutotepeyac.edu.mx*
Education Levels: preschool, primary, secondary, and high school

Instituto Tepeyac is an SEP-accredited traditional Mexican school that provides education to both national and foreign students. Its bilingual teaching system is based on a customized academic program meant to help each child develop their particular skills and aptitudes. Instituto Tepeyac Xcaret has a beautiful campus and is equipped with sports and artistic centers, multimedia halls, a pool, an American football and soccer field, and a cafeteria. The school also provides student transport.

Jardín de Niños Arte y Naturaleza Baaxal

Phone: 998 212 8188
Email: waldorfbaaxal@gmail.com
Website: *actiweb.es/waldorfbaaxal/*
Education Levels: preschool

This Waldorf-based school is located 30 minutes away from Playa del Carmen in Puerto Morelos and is a popular choice for parents who want their children to study in small classes and to enjoy a more personalized education. The campus is beautiful and has plenty of green space, and children are encouraged to spend their time outdoors.

Yits'Atil

Phone: 984 873 3874
Email: primaria_yitsatil@hotmail.com
Website: *yitsatil.edu.mx/yitsatil*
Education Levels: maternal, preschool, primary, secondary, and high school

Yits'Atil is an SEP school situated in downtown Playa del Carmen. It has a mixed student body of national and foreign students. The school offers a variety of extracurricular activities, including sports, dance, music, and yoga.

Public Institutions

City Hall

Phone: +52 984 877 3050
Website: solidaridad.gob.mx

Known by the locals as Palacio Municipal, the city hall of Playa del Carmen is the seat of the local government of Solidaridad, which governs the towns of Playa del Carmen, Paamul, Xpu-Ha, Puerto Aventuras and northern Akumal. This is the main administrative building in town and is the place where residents pay real estate property taxes and obtain both building permits and business licenses.

US Consular Agency

Phone: +52 984 873 0303; +52 984 807 8355 (emergency cell)
Email: pdcca.apointments@gmail.com

The US Consular Agency provides information and assistance to US citizens in Playa del Carmen, including passport renewals and replacements, notary services, and assistance in emergency matters such as arrest, crime, hospitalization, or death of a US citizen. However, since it doesn't have jurisdiction in Mexico, it can't interfere with local investigative and judicial procedures.

Dirección de Seguridad Publica y Tránsito Municipal

Phone: +52 984-877-3340

This is the Solidaridad Department of Public Safety and City Transit and is also the place where residents pay traffic tickets and apply for a driver's license.

Correos de Mexico

Phone: 52 984-873-0300; +01 800 701 4500 (toll-free in Mexico)

This is the local post office in Playa del Carmen.

PROFECO

Phone: +52 984 803 1261; +52 01 800 468 8722 (toll-free in Mexico)
Website: profeco.gob.mx

PROFECO is the consumer protection agency in Playa del Carmen and is the place where you can file a complaint about a local business. Most of the time, the mere mention of PROFECO to business owners is enough for them to do the right thing.

Community Institutions

Rotary Club of Playa del Carmen Seaside

Website: playaseasiderotary.org

Rotary Club is the English speaking branch of Rotary International in Playa del Carmen. The Rotary is a secular organization of business and professional leaders that provide humanitarian services and encourage high ethical standards. The Rotary Club in Playa del Carmen has 40 members representing North and South America, who seek to improve the daily lives and prospects of the children within the community.

Coco's Cat Rescue

Phone: +52 984 120 057
Website: cocoscatrescue.org

Coco's Cat Rescue is a rescue charity dedicated to spaying and neutering feral cats and to the care and re-homing of kittens in need of rescue. The charity provides free or low-cost spay and neuter surgeries, as well as vaccinations and basic animal care.

Playa Animal Rescue

Website: playaanimalrescue.org

This is a non-profit, no-kill animal shelter in Playa del Carmen, which focuses on rescuing and treating injured and abandoned dogs. They are also dedicated to finding permanent homes for each of the animals rescued.

Veterinarians

Clinica Veterinaria

Phone: +52 984 873 1108; +52 998 845 2498 (emergency)
Website: claudialewy.sitiosprodigy.mx

This clinic provides veterinary services and sells pet products.

Playa Pet

Phone: +52 984 873 0940; +52 998 112 2673 (emergency)
Email: playa_pet@yahoo.com
Website: facebook.com/playapet

Playa Pet specializes in orthopedic surgery on small animals. This clinic also sells pet products and accepts patients without appointments.

Religious Resources

While Mexican culture is predominantly Catholic, Mexicans are very tolerant of other religions and lifestyles, and a wide variety of religious services can be found in Playa. Expats living in Mexico enjoy the freedom to celebrate and embrace their faith without fear of judgement from others. There are many religious festivities in Mexico, and everyone is invited to enjoy the celebrations and find out more about their meaning and traditions.

Antioch Foursquare Christian Church

Phone: +52 984 130 4535,
Email: love4mexico@msn.com

This is a Christian Church, which holds English services every Sunday at 10:00 am. It is located in the south Ejido neighborhood.

Chabad-Lubavitch Jewish Center

Phone: +52 984 876 5571
Email: info@jewishplaya.com
Website: jewishplaya.com

Chabad-Lubavitch is a Jewish community center that offers daily and Shabbat services, kosher meals and, educational and social activities.

Diamond Way Buddhist Center

Phone: +52 984 806 4749
Website: budismo-playa.org

This is the only Buddhist center in Playa del Carmen.

Lighthouse Church Playa

Phone: +52 984 120 4163 (Pastor Dennis Teeters Mexico); +1 432 466 1044 (Pastor Dennis Teeters US and Canada); +52 984 593 3063 (Pastor Danny Delgado)

This is an English-speaking non-denominational Christian church.

Parroquia de Nuestra Señora del Carmen

Phone: +52 984 873 0188

Parroquia de Nuestra Señora del Carmen is a Catholic church.

Utilities

CFE Playa del Carmen

Email: servicioalcliente@cfe.gob.mx
Website: cfe.gob.mx

This is the government-owned company that provides electricity service in Playa del Carmen.

CAPA

Phone: +52 984 873 0286
Website: capa.gob.mx

CAPA is the place where those in Playa pay their water bills, set up new accounts, and modify their account details. This company treats and distributes water for the state of Quintana Roo. However, water bills can also be paid at any OXXO convenience store or online on the company's website.

Z Gas Plant

Phone: +01 800 011 ZETA
Website: grupozeta.com

Z Gas Plant is where people can go to get propane tanks filled in Playa.

Cablemás Chedraui

Phone: +52 984-873-3360; +52 984 873 3360; +01 800 522 2530 (toll-free in Mexico)
Website: cablemas.com

Cablemás Chedraui provides cable television and internet service.

Playa Wireless

Phone: +52 984 877 2390
Website: playawireless.com

This is the city's wireless internet service provider, which provides services in places where DSL and cable are not available.

Sys Digital Lab

Phone: +52 984 873 0132; +52 984 120 5325

Email: ventas@sysdigitallab.com
Website: sysdigitallab.com

This company offers satellite internet service, as well as computer supplies, accessories, repairs, security cameras, and website design services.

Telmex

Phone: +52 984 879 4689
Website: telmex.com.mx

This company specializes in telephone and internet service and is the only provider of land line telephone and DSL internet service in the Riviera Maya. Telmex also offers dial-up and wireless internet service.

Hospitals and Medical Clinics

Hospital San Carlos

Phone: +52 984 859 3313
Email: hospitalsancarlos@prodigy.net.mx
Website: hospitalsancarlos.com

This private hospital offers general medical assistance, as well as surgical and emergency care.

Hospiten Riviera Maya

Phone: +52 984 803 1002
Website: hospiten.com.mx/en/hospitales-y-centros/mexico-quintana-roo/hospiten-riviera-maya

Hospiten Riviera Maya offers a full range of medical services and various treatments.

MD Playa

Phone: +52 984 803 0648

Website: mdplaya.com

This modern clinic covers numerous specializations such as internal medicine, gynecology and obstetrics, cardiology, endocrinology, orthopedics, pediatrics, neonatology, plastic surgery, psychiatry, clinical nutrition, and nutrition for athletes. All the doctors speak English and on-call doctors are available after normal business hours.

Playa International Clinic

This clinic provides both routine doctor appointments and 24-hour emergency medical service. It is also equipped with a hyperbaric chamber and offers specialized medical care for commercial and recreational scuba divers. Its services include hospitalization, x-rays, laboratory, wound treatment, and a full service pharmacy.

Contact Information: +52 984 803 1215; emergency 24-hour: +52 984 873 1365, mdplaya.com

SANAR Clinic

Phone: +52 984 803 2039
Email: playarehabilitacionfisica@hotmail.com
Website: sanar.org.mx

SANAR Clinic welcomes its patients with services integrating both Western and Eastern medicine. Available services include acupuncture, ozone therapy, holistic therapy, aesthetic medicine, and family counseling.

Coral Dental Center

Phone: +52 984 803 1622; +52 984 876 2839 (emergency)
Email: info@coralcentalcenter.com
Website: coraldentalcenter.com/english/

This center provides full-service dental care, including surgical and cosmetic dentistry.

Dental Care Playacar

Phone: +52 984 803 2160; +52 984 113 4501
Email: info@coralcentalcenter.com

Dental care Playacar provides a variety of dental services, including special treatments like porcelain crowns, dental implants, and smile design.

Dr. Jorge Armenta

Phone: +52 984 873 2816
Email: gorgioso24@hotmail.com
Website: playadentist.com

This is a very popular dentist and dental surgeon in Playa del Carmen speaks fluent English.

Drugstores

Check Super Farmacia

Phone: 5515 87 90; 5515 88 90
Website: checksuperfarmacia.com

This full-service pharmacy sells prescription drugs, toiletries, liquor, and other small goods.

Derma SkinCare

Phone: +52 984 803 5673

This pharmacy specializes in hair and skincare products.

Farmacia del Ahorro

Phone: +52 984 803 089
Website: fahorro.com.mx

Farmacias Similares

Phone: +52 984 803 0091
Website: farmaciasdesimilares.com.mx

This pharmacy sells generic drugs and other low-cost health products and supplements. Every Monday, all products are discounted an additional 25%.

Fitness Facilities

B-Well Center

Phone: +52 984 803 1429b
Website: b-wellcenter.com/en

This kinesis and fitness studio is equipped with high tech equipment. Members have access to wellness programs and small group classes.

The Gym

Phone: +52 984 873 2098
Website: thegymplaya.com

This full-service gym is fitted with modern equipment and also has a pool. The Gym offers daily passes, weekly passes, and monthly memberships.

Legal Services

CHF Mexico Consulting

Phone: +52 984 803 4455
Email: info@chfmexico.com

CHF Mexico Consulting specializes in commercial, immigration, real estate, corporate, and family law.

Echavarría Manautou & Asociados

Phone: +52 984 803 2945; +52 984 803 2946
Email: echmanyasoc@hotmail.com

This legal office offers legal assistance in matters related to immigration, real estate, and incorporation.

Mendiola and Associates, P.C.

Phone: +52 984 873 3253; +52 984 132 4658
Email: tere_rubi_5@hotmail.com

This legal practice is run by a lawyer with over 30 years of experience in US and Mexican law. She specializes in immigration, real estate, criminal, and family law and is fluent in English, Spanish and French. The law firm also has access to a bilingual accounting and notary firm and certified in-house government translators.

Torres Pintos y Asociados

This office provides legal and accounting services.
Contact Information +52 984 859 3152; +52 984 879 6262

Vela Esperón Abogados, S.C.

Phone: +52 984 803 0396
Email: mdvq@velaesperon.com; contacto@velaesperon.com
Website: velaesperon.com

This law firm is served by 6 attorneys specializing in immigration, real estate, corporate, administrative, intellectual property, franchise, contract, and foreign investment law. They are also experienced in civil and mercantile litigation.

Arts and Entertainment

Teatro del Arbol

Website: facebook.com/teatro.delarbol

Teatro del Arbol is a small theater situated in the Parque la Ceiba. Participating in and watching local performances here is a great way to improve your language skills.

Cinemex

Phone: +52 984 803 9366; +52 984 803 9368
Website: cinemex.com

Situated at the Centro Maya shopping center, Cinemex is a modern multiplex movie theater, which screens many American movies with Spanish subtitles. Watching movies this way is another fun way to improve your language skills.

Cinépolis

Phone: +52 984 109 2114; 52 984 109 2121
Email: contacto@cinepolis.com.mx
Website: cinepolis.com

This is another multiplex movie theater that shows movies from the US and other countries in their original language accompanied by Spanish subtitles. This movie theater can be found at the Plaza Las Americas shopping center.

Comedy Playa

Phone: +52 1 984 106 0051
Website: comedyplaya.wordpress.com

This club features stand-up comedy in English. Playa del Carmen is often visited by comedians from the US, Canada, and the UK.

Centro Cultural Caracol Marino

Phone: +52 267 3136; +52 984 116 8439
Website: Centro-Cultural-Caracol-Marino

This is a non-profit organization dedicated to art and artists from various artistic fields.

Cultural Center Playa del Carmen

This is the official cultural center of the city.
Contact Information: facebook.com/direcciondecultura.solidaridad

Parks and Recreation

Parque 28 de Julio

Parque 28 de Julio is a gathering spot situated right across from Playa City Hall. It is a venue for many city events and is also the place where Playa's giant Christmas tree and nativity scenes are on display during the holiday season. This is a very popular area in the city, and it hosts a community recycling event every Friday. The park is located between Calles 10 and 8 and between 15th and 20th Avenues.

Parque Fundadores

This beautiful park is situated by the sea and includes gazebos, park benches, and a small playground for children. Parque Fundadores is located at Juarez Avenue between 5th Avenue and the sea.

Parque La Ceiba

This park rich has a number of attractions, including an art gallery, a small outdoor theater, a restaurant, and a children's playground. The park also has a recycling center and is a venue for various classes and special events. Parque La Ceiba also houses a crafts market on the third Saturday of each month. The park is located Av 1a Sur and Calle Diagonal 60.

Parque Leona Vicario

This recently renovated park has a basketball court and a climbing wall and is also a venue for occasional crafts markets. Parque Leona Vicario is located at 15th Avenue between Juarez Avenue and Calle 2.

Car Repairs

American Mechanic in Playa

Phone: +52 984 745 8509

An English-speaking auto mechanic named Roger has over 33 years of experience repairing a wide variety of cars (including both American-made cars and imports).

Carfix

Phone: +52 984 803 9520
Website: carfix.com.mx
This local business provides car repair services.

El Garage de Sam

Phone: +52 984 803 2494; +52 984 745 0219

Honda - Playa del Carmen

Phone: +52 984-877-2770

This is a Honda service office and car dealership in Playa.

Speed Service

Phone: 52 984-859-2856; +52 984-125-9141
Email: speedservice@live.com.mx

Speed service provides various car repair services.

Translation Services

Claudia Hurtado Valenzuela

Phone: +52 984 879 3228; +52 984 114 3868

Email: claudiadeplaya@hotmail.com

Claudia Hurtado Valenzuela is an interpreter and translator. She provides translations from English to Spanish and from Spanish to English. She also teaches Spanish for both beginners and advanced students.

Mendiola and Associates

Phone: +52 984 873 3253; +52 984 132 4658

Email: tere_rubi_5@hotmail.com

This law office also offers access to certified in-house government translators, who provide services in Dutch, English, French, German, Italian, Portuguese, and Spanish.

Riviera Maya Translations by Cisci

Email: csc78045@gmail.com

Cisci is a translator, who provides translation, editing, and proofreading services in English and Spanish. She also has experience in a variety of specialized areas, including medical terminology, general correspondence, web publicity, general advertising, newsletters, hotel directories, tourist information, menus, business cards, and invitations.

Car Rental Companies in Cancun and Playa del Carmen

Company	Website
Alamo	goalamo.com
Avicar	avicar.com.mx
Avis	avis.com
Caribetur	caribetur.com
Dollar	dollar.com
Europcar	europcar.com
Hertz	hertz.com
Mastercar	mastercar.com.mx
Monaco	monacorentacar.com
Payless	paylesscarrental.com
Qualitat	qualitatrentacar.com
Thrifty	thrifty.com.mx
Top	toprentacar.com

When driving in Playa del Carmen, pay attention to the one-way street system to avoid going the wrong way. Watch the traffic flow and drive defensively. If a police officer stops you, make sure to stay calm and be polite. Not many police officers speak English, so be patient.

By Taxi

Locals don't use taxis too often—not unless they are in a hurry or have luggage to carry. However, taxis can be found all over Playa del Carmen and are relatively inexpensive. They are usually compact cars that can provide transportation for up to 4 persons. Taxis can be hailed on the street or picked up at a taxi stand. You can also find many taxis waiting outside hotels.

Only a few taxi drivers in Playa speak English, so it's always a good idea to have your destination address written down. You should also ask for the cost of the ride before getting in the cab to avoid overcharging.

Taxis are not metered in Playa del Carmen; instead, their rates are fixed and can be found on a chart, which is displayed at the taxi stand on 10th Avenue and 12th Street. Most hotels also have a copy of the chart for their guests to consult.

Getting from Cancun Airport to Playa del Carmen

By Plane

Travelers, especially those coming from outside of Mexico, usually get to Playa by plane.

The Cancun International Airport is only a 45-minute drive from downtown Playa and offers hundreds of flights daily. You can also choose Cozumel International Airport and then take a ferry to Playa del Carmen.

Tip! Once you exit customs, you will be welcomed by many people eager to help you find your way to your hotel or house or even to carry your bags. While they may mean well, the safest thing to do is to ignore them.

By Bus

The cheapest way to get from the airport to Playa del Carmen is by bus. The airport is served by ADO bus company (+52 800 702 8000, ado.com.mx), which is also known as Riviera Bus. This bus service provides air conditioned rides from Cancun and Playa del Carmen. The bus service is reliable and efficient, and it provides multiple rides daily. The service from Cancun international airport is direct, and the only stops are downtown Cancun and downtown Playa. The entire trip takes about 65 minutes.

Directions to the Bus Station: If you are flying from the US to Cancun, you will probably land at Terminal 3. If you do, you should turn left down the hallway after going through immigration and customs. After you pass the rental car offices, you should see the ADO stand, where you can buy a bus ticket. The bus to Playa del Carmen usually departs from Platform 2, but a digital sign on the front should tell you the destination for each bus.

If you land at Terminal 2, turn right after exiting your terminal. After walking the length of the building, you will come to a security gate, where you will be able to see the bus station.

Terminal 1 is only used for domestic flights, but if you arrive there, you will need to take the free airport shuttle to one of the other terminals before you can get to bus.

Note! The seating is open, even if the ticket has a seat number. However, you should still keep the bus ticket on you for the entire journey in case you need to present it.

Tip! You can also buy your bus tickets online. Online reservations come with a guaranteed seat. When you buy tickets this way, an airport representative will wait for you outside of your arrival terminal and will take you to the bus stop.

By Taxi

Authorized taxis can be found at the taxi stations situated outside of the arrival terminal. A trip from Cancun to Playa by private taxi takes about 45 minutes and typically costs about $65. When travelling by taxi, it's always a good idea to carry small bills and change. You should also keep in mind that most taxi drivers in Mexico don't speak English.

Getting from Playa del Carmen to Cancun International Airport

By Bus

The buses for Cancun International Airport depart from the 5th Avenue and Juarez bus station also stop at Playa's 20th Street station. After leaving Playa del Carmen, the bus doesn't stop until it reaches the airport terminals.

Note! Make sure you arrive at the airport at least an hour before your flight. If you can, check in online to save time too. You should also be careful not to lose your travel documents, especially if you are travelling with children!

By Private Transfer

If you prefer more comfort and privacy or if you're traveling with a group, then booking a private transfer is a great option. The companies that offer these transfers have air-conditioned vehicles in a variety of sizes, and they are often quicker than buses since they don't make added stops.

Companies that Provide Private Airport Transfers:

ESL Transfers (+011 52 998 2061085; + 011 52 998 2940135, esltransfers.com)

Dream Days (US Toll-Free: 1 888 233 2156; 1 305 615 0554; Mexico Toll-Free from Land Lines: +01-800-681-9340, dreamdays.com)

Entertainment Plus (From US: +011 52 998 914 0290; 310 909 8634; from Cancun: +914 0290; from the Riviera Maya: +09 998 914 0290; from a Mexican Cell Phone: +044 998 195 5491, entertainment-plus.net)

By Shuttle Van

Shuttle vans don't leave at specific hours; instead, their departure time depends on when they have enough passengers for a profitable trip. While they can be convenient, these shuttles often stop at many hotels and resorts, which slows down the trip.

> **Note!** Always purchase tickets from an official TTC kiosk instead of from any individuals selling tickets outside.

Dining Out

Dining in Playa can be a lot of fun and is a great way to get to know the city. Since Playa attracts so many tourists, it has plenty of restaurants, cafes, and eateries for residents to choose from.

The establishments located in the tourist areas (and especially along 5th Avenue) tend to have English menus and English-speaking waiters. Unfortunately, these places also have American prices and are not the most affordable.

Generally speaking, the farther you are from 5th Avenue you go, the cheaper your meal will be. To get a taste of the authentic Mexican food, you should leave the touristic areas and head to the core of Playa del Carmen. Mexican restaurants can easily be found if you walk up Juarez Avenue to 30th Avenue and then head north.

Mexican food is extremely diverse, and you should definitely try to experience as much of it as you can. *Comida corrida* (street food) is especially good in Playa and is a great way to experience authentic Mexican food without spending much. *Antojitos* (little appetizers) are sold almost everywhere. Popular *antojitos* include tamales, gorditas, quesadilla, tostadas, and tortas.

> **Tip!** When dining at a restaurant, it isn't unusual for strangers to say *"provecho"* (enjoy your meal) to others tables as they are leaving. If someone says this to you, *"gracias"* is the appropriate reply.

The restaurants listed below are places where you can get a great meal for 100 pesos (about $7) or less. They may not be as fancy as some of the tourist traps in town, but they are just as (if not more) delicious!

Restaurant Name	Type of Cuisine	Location
Chez Celine	French Breakfast and Lunch	5th Avenue and Calle 34
Comida Casera	Homemade Food and Breakfast	25th Avenue and Calle 6
Chimi Churri	Argentinian	Calle 6 between 10th and 15th Avenue
Café Guajira	Sandwiches and Burgers	Calle 6 between 15th and 20th Avenue
Guacamoles	Mexican	10th Avenue between Calles 8 and 10
Dona Paula Restaurant	Mexican	Calle 6 between 10th and 15th Avenue
Mi Kfe	Venezuelan	10th Avenue between Calles 6 and 8
Euro Grill	Grill Favorites	East Side of 5th Avenue
Antojitos Playa del Carmen	Native Mexican Dishes	30th Avenue between Calles 2 and 4
Burro Playero	Burritos	Calle 8 between 10th and 15th Avenues and Inside Centro Maya
Old Burrito	Burritos	Calle 32 between 5th and 10th Avenues
Vaca Loca	Hamburgers and Fries	Corner of 15th Avenue and Calle 8
Mr. Kiwi	Burgers, Sandwiches, and Smoothies	Between Calles 8 and 10
Loco Joe	**Burgers and Sandwiches**	**30th Avenue**
La Brocherie	French Food and Paninis	15th Avenue between Calles 4 and 6
El Pechugon	Roast Chicken	Corner of 10th Avenue
El Rey	Tacos	Calle 14bis between the Mega

		and Aki Supermarkets on 30th Avenue
Tacon Tenedor	Seafood Tacos	Constituyentes Avenue, between 5th and 10th Avenue
Tacos Arabes	Mediterranean-Inspired Tacos	Calle 8 between 15th and 20th Avenue
El Fogon	Tacos	30th Avenue between Calles 6 and 8 and at Constituyentes Avenue between 25th and 30th Avenue
Don Sirloin	Tacos	10th Avenue between Calles 12 and 14 and at Constituyentes Avenue and 25th Avenue
Juana Cortez's Taco Truck	Tacos	Calle 14bis between 30th and 35th Avenue (near the Mega Supermarket)
Mama Mia Pizza	Pizza	Calle 2 between 10th and 15th Avenue and at 10th Avenue between Calles 8 and 10
Comedor La Victoria	Mexican	Calle 22 between 5th and 10th Avenue

Nightlife and Clubbing

Playa's nightlife is vibrant, and those who want to party all night long are free to do so. Playa's wide variety of bars includes quiet bars, bars with trees, sports bars, bars with live music, beach bars, and more. While most bars in Playa close at 2 am, many of the night clubs are open until 4 or later. Also, most nightclubs and bars are free to enter, so you will only be charged for what you order.

Important! Drinking open containers of alcohol on the street is prohibited in Playa.

Many of Playa's clubs are located on or near 5th Avenue, but there are other options in other areas of Playa as well.

There are also a number of bars and clubs lining Playa's beaches, which are a perfect place to dance the night away while enjoying the scenery.

Tip! Mexicans, both friends and casual acquaintances, sometimes kiss each other on the cheek in greeting. Expats may find this a bit confusing at first, but the custom should be easy for them to adjust to over time

---

The following rules for kissing in greeting will make it easier for expats to adjust to life in Playa.

- Always kiss someone on the right cheek.

- Usually, kissing is practiced woman to woman and woman to man, but not man to man (unless the men are family members).

- Women usually make the first move when kissing a man's cheek.

- When greeting a casual acquaintance, it's enough to just touch cheeks and kiss the air.

- Mexicans sometimes kiss someone on the cheek the first time they meet them (rather than shake their hand).

Public Holidays in Mexico

January

January 1: *Ano Nuevo* (New Year's Day)

January 6: *Dia de Los Santos Reyes* is the day when Mexicans exchange Christmas presents in accordance with the day when the 3 gift-bearing wise men visited Jesus Christ. This day marks the end of Mexican Christmastime festivities.

January 17: The Feast Day of San Antonio de Abad is a religious holiday, during which the Catholic Church allows animals to enter the church for blessing.

February

February 2: *Dia de la Candelaria* (Candlemas) is a religious holiday that is celebrated with processions, dancing, and the blessing of the seeds and candles. Some cities also celebrate with bullfights.

February 5: *Dia de la Constitucion* is an official holiday that commemorates Mexico's Constitution.

February 26 to March 4 (approximately): *Carnaval* is an official Mexican holiday that involves a 5-day celebration of the libido before Catholic Lent. *Carnaval* begins the weekend before Lent and is celebrated exuberantly with parades, floats, and dancing in the streets. Port towns such as Cozumel, Ensenada, La Paz, Mazatlán, and Veracruz are excellent places to watch the *Carnaval* festivities.

February 24: Flag Day is national Mexican holiday that honors the Mexican flag.

March

March 18: *La Expropiacion Petrolera* is a civic holiday marking the Oil Expropriation of March 18, 1938.

March 19: *Dia de San Jose* (St. Joseph's Day), a religious holiday that's best celebrated in in Tamuin, San Luis Potosi.

March 21: The Birthday of Benito Juarez is a holiday honoring the famous Mexican President and national hero Benito Juarez.

April

Semana Santa: *Semana Santa* is the holy week that ends the 40-day Lent period. This week includes Good Friday and Easter Sunday. It is Mexican custom to break confetti-filled eggs over the heads of friends and family during this time.

May

May 1: *Primero de Mayo* is a national Mexican holiday that is a lot like Labor Day in the US.

May 3: *Dia de la Santa Cruz* (Day of the Holy Cross) is a day on which construction workers decorate and mount crosses on unfinished buildings. The day is also celebrated with fireworks and picnics at construction sites.

May 5: *Cinco de Mayo* is the national Mexican holiday that honors the Mexican victory over the French army in 1862.

May 10: Mother's Day is an especially significant holiday in Mexico, because mothers are an extremely important part of Mexican Culture.

June

June 1: Navy Day

June 24: Saint John the Baptist Day is celebrated with religious festivities and fairs.

June 29: Fiesta of Saint Peter and Saint Paul

September

September 1 (approximately): The State of the Union is given in the fall. The President gives his annual address to the nation.

September 13: *Los Niños Héroes* (Heroes of the Mexican-American War) is the day on which the President of Mexico commemorates those who fought during the Mexican-American War with a wreath-laying ceremony at the monument to *Los Niños Héroes* in Chapultepec Park.

September 16: Mexican Independence Day celebrates the day that Miguel Hidalgo delivered *El Grito de Dolores* and announced the Mexican revolt against Spanish rule.

October

October 12: *Día de la Raza* is a day marking Columbus's arrival to the Americas and the historical origins of the Mexican race.

November

November 1-2: *Día de los Muertos* (Day of the Dead) is an important Mexican holiday that merges Pre-Columbian beliefs with modern Catholicism. The day is meant to honor Mexico's dead.

November 20: Mexican Revolution Day commemorates the Mexican Revolution of 1910.

December

December 12: *Día de Nuestra Senora de Guadalupe* (The Day of the Virgin of Guadalupe) is celebrated with feasting and honors Mexico's patron saint.

December 16-January 6: *Las Posadas* celebrates Joseph and Mary's search for shelter in Bethlehem with candlelight processions that end at various nativity scenes.

December 25: *Navidad* is Mexico's Christmas holiday.

Learning Spanish: Resources for Expats

Spanish is the official language in Mexico, and even though many people in Playa do speak English, you should still make some effort to learn Spanish if you plan to stay in the country for longer than a few months. You may be able to get by as an expat without knowing any Spanish, but you won't be able to truly immerse yourself in Playa's culture or get to know its people. Knowing conversational Spanish is also a must if you plan to get a job in Mexico.

Mexicans appreciate it when expats take the time to try to learn Spanish, so don't be afraid to ask locals any language questions that you might have.

There are many Spanish language schools in Playa del Carmen that help expats learn the language much more quickly than they could on their own.

Academia Columbus

Website: http://www.academia-columbus.com.

Situated only a few minutes away from the beach, Academia Columbus offers a beautiful setting for learning Spanish. The classes take place in thatched roof cabins surrounded by a beautiful exotic garden dotted with palm trees. The school also has a lovely patio with a volleyball court, a cafeteria, and a balcony.

International House Riviera Maya

Website: http://ihrivieramaya.com.

This school is situated only 30 meters from 5th Avenue and 2 blocks from the beach. The school has a beautiful garden, a cafeteria, a computer lab, and a library. It also offers free access to wireless internet and a suite of language-learning software.

Solexico Language and Cultural Centers

Website: http://www.solexico.com.

Founded in 1997, this is one of the most reputable Spanish language schools in Playa del Carmen. Solexico is located 6 blocks away from the beach and has a cafeteria, computer lab, library, movie room, volleyball court, and a lovely garden. The school also offers facilities for disabled students.

Berlitz

Website: http://berlitzplayadelcarmen.com.

Berlitz offers Spanish courses based on the world-famous Berlitz method. The school offers private, semi-private, and group classes, as well as TOEFL preparation courses. Classes can be taken live, online, or as part of a combined learning program.

Playalingua del Caribe

Website: http://playalingua.com.

Playalingua del Caribe was founded more than 10 years ago and was one of the first language schools to teach Spanish in Playa del Carmen. This small, independent school offers personalized instruction and offers a beautiful and relaxing learning environment. Playalingua del Caribe is located only 5 minutes away from the beach and 5th Avenue. Breakfast is served in the school's cafeteria.

Sprachhcaffee
Website: http://www.sprachcaffe.com.
The Sprachhcaffee Spanish school welcomes students with a vast array of classes that are suitable for everyone. The school even offers quick 2-week language courses as well as individual lessons for all levels. The school has a large outdoor swimming pool, a restaurant, a roof terrace, and a tour office.

Language Studies International (Partner School)
Phone: +1 619 564 5450
Website: http://www.lsi.edu/en.
The LSI Partner School offers Spanish courses in open air classrooms situated in an enchanting tropical garden. Classes are capped at 5 students each, and all students have access to unlimited wireless access and the school's multimedia lab.

Index

T

U

V

W

About the Expat Fever Series

Are you ready for a major lifestyle change? The Expat Fever Series is all about the demystifying the expat journey. If you want to start fresh in a new country and immerse yourself in a new culture but aren't sure where to start, our books are packed with information that should help put you on the right path. Our books are meant to give readers a sense of what it's really like to live in a specific area, and all of them include candid interviews with real expats, who discuss both the pros and the cons of their expat journey.

Millions of people are deciding to move to a new country, but is expatriating right for you? Read the *Expat Fever!* series and find out for yourself!

Get more information and sign up for travel tips at:

http://www.expatfever.com.

Made in the USA
Las Vegas, NV
19 July 2021